En Abîme: Listening, Reading, Writing

An archival fiction

www.danielacascella.com
enabime.wordpress.com

En Abîme: Listening, Reading, Writing

An archival fiction

Daniela Cascella

Winchester, UK
Washington, USA

First published by Zero Books, 2012
Zero Books is an imprint of John Hunt Publishing Ltd., Laurel House, Station Approach,
Alresford, Hants, SO24 9JH, UK
office1@jhpbooks.net
www.johnhuntpublishing.com
www.zero-books.net

For distributor details and how to order please visit the 'Ordering' section on our website.

Text copyright: Daniela Cascella 2011

ISBN: 978 1 78099 403 1

A CIP catalogue record for this book is available from the British Library.

Design: Stuart Davies

Printed and bound by CPI Group (UK) Ltd, Croydon, CR0 4YY

We operate a distinctive and ethical publishing philosophy in all
areas of our business, from our global network of authors to
production and worldwide distribution.

CONTENTS

Foreword

En abîme is compulsive and fast, rushing with you through textual territories that seem spoken, direct and contemporary while being nostalgic - invoking a past that creates the present tense. It produces a wonderful séjourne into history that brings with it the contemporary condition of being, remote, apart, unseen, but in constant contact. Its words compose a listening journey that reminds of diaries written before the computer and the internet: crafted by hand, meticulously inscribing every shard of the traveller's experience and thought. And so it talks intriguingly about listening to culture and cultural artefacts, not to know about sound but to know about culture, the social, the political and to make you understand rather than know the 'expanding function of listening'.

I read its voice aloud in my mind. A strong single narrating voice that is dispersed but not distracted, connecting in sound the circumstance of now as a fluent stream of poetry, philosophy, fiction, description and reverie.

Salomé Voegelin

Acknowledgments

My first thank you is to my very early readers, Helena Hunter and Mark Peter Wright, whose tireless response to my drafts and whose long-term involvement with this project were a vital force throughout.

I am very grateful to Chiara Guidi, Paolo Inverni, Adrian Rifkin, Sarah Tripp and Richard Whitelaw for supporting my work, and to Maria Fusco at Goldsmiths, University of London for her insight into the editing process.

Thank you to Lou Mallozzi at the School of the Art Institute of Chicago for giving me the chance to present my first public reading from the manuscript of *En abîme* at the *Sound Art Theories* symposium; to Cathy Lane and Angus Carlyle at CRiSAP, University of the Arts London and Helen Frosi at SoundFjord for commissioning texts which were later reworked into sections of this book.

In particular I would like to thank Chiara O. Bertola for reading and responding to the early chapters of this book with warmth and understanding; Tone Gellein for sharing many conversations and for listening when most needed; Stefano Scalich who offered significant editorial advice and challenged me to push my words to the edge; Maria Paola Zedda for a trip to via Appia one day in August; all the artists mentioned in these pages.

I am profoundly thankful to three writers and artists whose approach to listening and writing gave me a sense of context and whose support at various stages of this book was crucial. David Toop read the manuscript and responded positively to the writing early on. His book *Sinister Resonance*, a compelling study of sound in silent media, was a major inspiration for me to combine art, sound, poetry and literature; in countless articles and readings his understanding of the multifaceted nature of listening opened up the discourse around sound to a range of references and disciplines, not restricted to the specificity of a medium. My dialogue with Steve Roden for over a decade was essential to the shaping of this book, even before I set out to write it. His encouraging comments to my early drafts urged me to stay true to the writing; his reflections on listening as a connecting activity, alongside a shared interest in the language of fiction and of poetry as means to articulate and ingrain listening experiences, fuelled *En abîme* in more ways than I could possibly list. Salomé Voegelin's unique vision and drive, although encountered at a late point in my research, were a spur for clarity. Her radical positioning of listening, in her book *Listening to Noise and Silence* and in her blog soundwords.tumblr.com, offered an intense counterpoint to my reflections and a challenge to think forward. Salomé was the last person who read my manuscript, so it is fitting that her voice appears as a foreword of *En abîme*, as yet another echo of its polyphonic structure.

This book wouldn't exist without the generosity and trust of my brother Michele and my parents Nina and Vincenzo.

Most of all, thank you to Colin for being there always.

Part 1

CHAPTER 1

A POSTCARD FROM ETHEL

1.

In February 1998 I received a postcard from Ethel B.:

Monday, February 9th, 1998
Very dear D.,
I have supreme confidence in you.
Baziotes and I loved the Roman wall paintings in the Metropolitan – we returned to them again and again.
Stay close to Leonardo, Giorgione and St. Francis who loved the harp.
I hold your hand.
Love, Ethel B.
Persevere – Stay close to the abyss.

2.

In February 1998 I received a postcard from Ethel B. with whom I'd engaged, through the first half of the previous year, in an absorbing though unusual dialogue. When I was in New York to research my University dissertation, somebody had suggested I get in touch with her as she might have documents, and insights, relevant to my studies.

Ethel and I in fact never met. For months we spoke for hours over the phone.

I can't recall many details of what we discussed. I remember that soon all study-oriented questions were left aside, and our conversations became animated by connections between seeing and reading, poetry and painting – unexpected and electric. It was not synaesthesia but cohabitation of worlds, which existed because we would weave our stories around them: so the rhythm of a verse and the gleaming fixity of a lizard's eye would seep into a certain painting, into our reading of a certain painting.

Ethel was in her eighties, but she still lived in the forties and fifties. I could sense it in the way she talked of people and of places: she'd kept them with her all those years, as a silent presence. I remember her voice: a cloud of vaporous vowels and edgeless consonants, that made each pause shimmer. It carried a thread of words on the verge of breaking down.

If the quality of Ethel's voice was frail, the intent behind it was firm. It was her voice, which halved Ethel's time into the time of her most vivid memories. It came from somebody who knew she was close to the end, and kept a connection to her memories and the emotions within them, which got stronger in remembrance as their physical counterpart faded out.

For the entire stretch of my stay in New York, Ethel and her voice talked me into an elsewhere. Often I would resonate with her words although I felt like a guest inside them. As I listened, I was confronted with the early manifestations of a hidden impression that would be disclosed in the rest of my work and my words in years to come. This I knew then: words, sounds, art did not want to be understood. They wanted to get close, and just be there. Curl up against me and be: as texture and experience. They were to be with me, not as a mild habit but as an addiction.

My memories disappear into Ethel's voice. Soon before I left New York, she sent me a book of poems by Emily Dickinson. I recall the first verses my eyes fell upon, *it sounded as if the streets were running, and then the streets stood still.* These words seemed to foresee a vision embedded in sound, an insistence on a singular landscape drawn by streets, by slivers of light, by the interplay of motion and stillness, looked upon from a very singular window. It was made of words resonating, heard, recalled; of voices translated, embodied, recorded.

3.

Monday, February 9th, 1998

Very dear D.,

I have supreme confidence in you.

Baziotes and I loved the Roman wall paintings in the Metropolitan – we returned to them again and again.

Stay close to Leonardo, Giorgione and St. Francis who loved the harp.

I hold your hand.

Love, Ethel B.

Persevere – Stay close to the abyss.

Those words, arranged in such a manner; a postcard from somebody I'd never met, but who seemed to know me nonetheless. I felt connected.

Of the whole postcard, it was not the mention of Leonardo and Giorgione that struck me most. I was not familiar then with any links between St. Francis and the harp. I'd learned of perseverance a long way back, and I was close enough to the edge of a personal abyss to believe Ethel was not joking there. What made me think, what stayed with me throughout the years, was the reference to the wall paintings.

The display of the Roman wall paintings at the Metropolitan Museum in New York is a striking combination of museological marvel and sensuous wonder. I walk in the reconstructed spaces of the *Black Room* of the Imperial Villa at Boscotrecase; of the Villa of P. Fannius Synistor at Boscoreale. Or, shall I spell Sinister? My eyes move along the walls. They follow the thin white lines of the elaborate architectural constructions depicted in the Black Room paintings: flimsy painted pillars supporting pavilions, candelabra, jewel-encrusted slabs. All around, I see little swans in a precarious balance on spiralling coils. Hovering in the middle, miniature landscapes are glued onto the recesses of the black background. I search for vertigo in this absolute flatness. I see silent figurines in rigid poses, near-black blue against the agony of these clouds; patiently woven garlands, flowers mutating into gems, marbles and hard stones.

Walking on, my eyes fall into Polyphemus' eye, a tiny point of chalky white against a vast background of deep green and blue. I wonder if my vertigo can be resolved in this eye. I see red, black, brushes of gesso white: blocks of them. Gilded decorations, flashes of light. Edges and undecipherable arabesques. A sense of charged presence. A clash of sharp geometry and sinewy lines, one exceeding the other yet embracing one another in circling motion. I hear an apparition and its colour is white. Out of this perennial darkness a sparkle gleams, in my vision hours upon hours pulverise into dust, these figures compose themselves in a parade of death, I hear an explosion far away then all is silent, as a gathering of dusty clouds looms over these fake horizons. I hear an apparition and its colour is white. That little eye, that little point of white now swells up and precipitates in my vision and it makes the blackness flourish again like a new cloud, then it discloses a sun shedding light all over. A luminous nebula of tiny points drizzles like a warm rain, it falls all over the thin white columns until a veil of dark and powder covers all, unforgiving.

Polyphemus: my many-voiced, much-heard-of sight. I hear an apparition and its colour is white.

4.

On the front of Ethel's postcard is a reproduction of *Dwarf*, a 1947 painting by her late husband William Baziotes. Striking tones of acid green and pink, vapours heavily charged by Baudelairean reveries, out of which in thin slate-grey lines a creature emerges. It nearly occupies the entirety of the canvas, it looks like it wants to absorb it all in its struggle to be – embracing, despite its thinness. It is made just by a few lines and illuminated by a phosphorescent, sulphuric green. It is just one lump of matter, no limbs are visible, or maybe they were mutilated. The mouth, a zigzagged expressionless grin. To the right, one big eye looks at me and counters another eye, made of concentric circles on the lower side of the canvas. Polyphemus: one-eyed, many-voiced, much-heard-of sight.

I revisit this relic from the past and my words embark on a journey across its surface, as I scan voices and stillness and as they think through me – or it is I thinking through them *but musically and pictorially, without witticisms, without syllogisms, without deductions*, as Baudelaire would have it and as Ethel would recall in her keen reading of the French poet, prompting her husband to paint. So what unspoken stories lie behind this creature of green and pink and subtle lines of web and stone, and what do I hear? And where does this eye take me, caught between listening and daydreaming? The closer I get, the more this picture looks immense and remote. Just like the figures against the background in the *Black Room* at the Metropolitan Museum. A subtle hum creeps as this surface becomes crammed with it. I begin to hear words of mutilation.

At the time they appeared, Harold Rosenberg wrote of an appeasing vibration flowing through the colours in Baziotes' paintings and their pigments, whose textures seem to absorb silence *as if they'd been mixed in a medium of sleep*. It's been said this picture is eerie. It's been written about the disquieting innocence of this fixed gaze, its slowly unfolding evil glance out of a stubborn stillness. As I look, its gaze looks more sorely devoid, more blatantly still. I see fixity in this Grünewald green: I see the wooden rigidity of these mutilated limbs. As I focus I hear a tune, flowing gently from some remote regions of the mind. At first it seems hushed, an undercurrent reappearing from the past; it then becomes denser, hovering like a cloud of harmonics dancing around a single note. It reaches impossible heights of pitch; it hums like a swarm of bees. It then thins out to a single voice that charms me in its coils then moves backwards again, far away. Initially I can't single out any words: just a sweet moan which takes on the shape of a beastly groan, of a sinister dirge. The trace of a primitive force seeps through this portrait of marbled stillness. It arises from the voice of stone and web of my memory, as I think and feel through this surface.

Disguised in the voice of my personal Siren, I begin to hear a song. It is entitled *Il testamento del capitano, The Captain's Testament.*

5.

... body of a slain comrade, mouth snarling ... fingers ripping into my silence...

6.

I recall the words on the previous page, echoing those written by the Italian poet Giuseppe Ungaretti when he was a soldier in World War I.

One of Baziotes' sources for his *Dwarf* was the image of a mutilated World War I veteran.

The Captain's Testament is part of a collection of Alpine chants from World War I, sung a cappella by one of the many traditional choirs from Northern Italy. It sings of a mutilation of sorts. The captain of a company is mortally wounded and asks his soldiers to cut his body into five pieces: one for Italy, his homeland, one for the company, one for his mother, one for his love and the last one for the mountains, that will cover it with roses and flowers.

Covered by flowers, daisies and anemones, I begin to recall a burial ground in Rome.

7.

In Rome today I return to via Appia. Across trains shrieking and crowds rumbling in the streets, across the uneven rhythm of sirens, across the roar of engines, the ceaseless hissing of people's iPods stretching like filigree, across the coarse texture of the city noise, a train of thoughts unwinds along my journey, where other voices begin to take shape.

Walking on via Appia today, I thought I'd found the contours of what I was seeking.

With great lucidity I recall a certain painting from the sixteenth century and with it the stupor that overcame me when I first saw it in a book at school. A *Deposizione, Deposition*: my eyes first encounter those of the young man who holds not just the heavy body of Christ, but the entire composition. No cross appears in the picture: this painter always hides the props. It seems that he does not need any architectural or structural grip in order to state his vision. All exists on the surface. The sky is defined only by a little cloud; only by a pale bit of ground, the earth. The colours one would expect in a landscape are transposed within the shapes of people: not only in their clothes but also in their skin, as if to reinforce the flatness of this surface and the non-hierarchical arrangement of its patterns. A face is scarlet as the burning of a silent fever, another yellowy green as of dry leaves. Pallid, pastel, pain-stricken poses seem to fix these figures in a cloud of melancholy rather than in the pangs of loss. Only their glances flee. No angular lines: all is soft curves, yet caught in unnatural poses. The modulation of hues and tones calls for focus and displaces. The contours do not constitute the volume of the forms, but prevent them from gaining volume. This is not painting and movement, this does not hint at sculpture and monumental balance. Classical forms here are devoid of any depth; they exist in their spiralling rhythm. This picture is resolved in the tempo of its shapes and this is a painter of visual poems.

Chapter 1

The figure of Christ is bent in a double curve and swollen. His torso, a lump of pink flesh. The face is not that of an eruptive cadaver but of a still body. Against a barely-there sky, at some point this entire surface seems to bow down, almost to lean toward me. None of the ten figures in the scene, spiralling, none of them keeps watch over Christ: either their eyes are averted, or they look at me out of the surface, stuck in their impossibility of roundedness. The Virgin wears a cloak of the colour of the sky: there is no real sky in this painting, the sky is in her cloak. She is stuck pensive in her hushed lyricism. Maybe she is just about to sob.

8.

The *Deposition* by Pontormo, kept in the church of Santa Felicita in Florence, was revisited by Pier Paolo Pasolini in a tableaux vivant featured in his short film *La ricotta*, shot in a site off via Appia in Rome.

In Pontormo's painting each face and each figure is arranged within the logic of the plane and evened out in an appearance of sublime grief. In Pasolini's film the sublime grief descends back to earth and the flatness gains volume out of the manners and the expressions of the people enacting the scene: the poor, the prostitute, the rich actress, the old man, all with their faces and postures, most of all with their direct presence. Human, and yet removed: *La ricotta* is a short film staging the shooting of a film, where the representation of the Passion of Christ is interwoven with the story of hungry Stracci, an extra who ends up being crucified – both literally, and symbolically. Orson Welles plays the film director, Pasolini's actors of choice play the real people who play the saints and the real people in the Passion, the Roman suburbs play a scenario of golden stillness.

Be still! Be still!, shouts the voice of the director to the people in the film, who are staging the tableaux vivant reproducing Pontormo's painting. *You can't move, you are the figures in an altarpiece!* And yet they move; and yet the close-ups of the camera capture their most human gestures, they pry on the moments where hieratic poses merge into ordinary expressions, where solemnity is touched by distraction. Then the entire construction falls down, clumsy, and everyone laughs. Pasolini's oxymoronic vision spans the two extremes; it distils the innermost essence of human nature into a glimpse of beauty, soon to be corrupted and to fall apart. In his representation of Pontormo's painting he reveals the tangible and the unspeakable together, as one shakes the other in a vision of stillness before crumbling down. *These images are at once, grand and real. At once sublime, and of earth earthy.*

9.

Typical Roman-noon white light. Metallic noise. *Shall we descend? Let's go.* Haze and dust and more noise. *The underground of Rome is unpredictable. Here the underground is made of eight layers. We are not just builders, we need to mutate into archaeologists, into speleologists.* Tunnels underground. *We are now travelling underneath the Appio quarter.* Tunnels coiling down. Clangour. *We are under via Appia Antica, near Porta San Sebastiano.* A row of people wear red helmets, faces covered. *Here is a necropolis with four hundred skeletons.* Third layer. The clangour thins down to a hiss. Then a roar again. *Another void cave has been found.* Deafening noise. *It is a very big void that's been detected.* I HEAR AN APPARITION AND ITS COLOUR IS WHITE. The hand of the engineer touches the wall and probes it intently. *Start the milling cutter.* A high-pitched engine noise is repeated in a stubborn pattern. The milling cutter looms. OUT OF THIS PERENNIAL DARKNESS A SPARKLE GLEAMS, IN MY VISION HOURS UPON HOURS PULVERISE INTO DUST, THESE FIGURES COMPOSE THEMSELVES IN A PARADE OF DEATH, I HEAR AN EXPLOSION FAR AWAY THEN ALL IS SILENT, AS A GATHERING OF DUSTY CLOUDS LOOMS OVER THESE FAKE HORIZONS. I HEAR AN APPARITION AND ITS COLOUR IS WHITE. Now the camera shows an underground cave immersed in whitish light, in contrast with the earth-coloured hall where the workers stand. The engineer seems to faint. Ancient wall paintings all around. SOMETIMES, FROM THE FRESCOES AND PAINTINGS, THEIR FACES STARE AT US. FROM BOOKS THOUGH, YOU HARDLY EVER HEAR THEIR VOICES. As the milling cutter drills a hole, a gust of wind hisses through the void halls. *A Roman house, from two thousand years ago! Down.* Descend. Still white sculptures, a hiss again. A procession of figures is pictured on one of the walls. A mosaic face on the floor, underneath a shallow pool of water. Half-cracked faces loom from the vaults. Those faces stare at us as they are being stared at. A moment of recognition. The faces in the wall paintings begin to dissolve. The air from outside destroys the paintings, up to that point preserved in the balanced air of their being locked in. *Do something, do something!* The faces dissolve into a dusty whitish blue. THAT LITTLE POINT OF WHITE NOW SWELLS UP AND PRECIPITATES IN MY VISION AND IT MAKES THE BLACKNESS FLOURISH AGAIN LIKE A NEW CLOUD, THEN IT DISCLOSES A SUN SHEDDING LIGHT ALL OVER. A LUMINOUS NEBULA OF TINY POINTS DRIZZLES LIKE A WARM RAIN, IT FALLS ALL OVER THE THIN WHITE COLUMNS UNTIL A VEIL OF DARK AND POWDER COVERS ALL, UNFORGIVING. I HEAR AN APPARITION AND ITS COLOUR IS WHITE. Then the hiss of the wind only, and I'm watching Federico Fellini's *Roma*.

And I'm watching Rome. Melting lights and bursting knots of noise: November. On a damp late November day I descend to meet more wall paintings, in the Domus Aurea. As I walk down, I feel close to something from which I'd kept away. Gone is the time of hiding. *Stay close to the abyss.* A forceful movement arises from the past, a vortex jolts out of a primordial eye in this cave. All the rest now has to do with living up to this, close to the abyss. I heard an apparition and its colour was black. Have you ever seen the edges of these figures? Have you ever seen their eyes? They form a fraying frame, an ersatz reminder of rotting icons, with no edge other than these walls. Their faces scream bordello. They disappear beneath the surface. I heard an apparition and its colour was black. Ghosts in this hall, a dome inside. And as the howling and the screaming clear away of this heavy night, I hear the pace of a slow *Kyrie* unfold. My words record the eroding howl, its closely muffled verse. Animal verse, outside verse. I heard an apparition and its colour was black. Its hiss is on my heels calling for me, calling me out of this dead city of tombs. This dead city of tombs is chasing me, I walk. Up to this very moment walking, listening, recalling.

10.

Going out, to the surface, I think of Henri David Thoreau and of one point of *Walden* in which he wrote that, no matter where he found himself, in his walks he always headed West. My words and my walks always point South-East. As I exit the Domus Aurea I look over the pine trees down toward via Appia, across dishevelled Mediterranean shrubs, as if the only way out was my sense of direction, while the rest crumbles away to a pre-language made of hiss, gushes and half-guessed formulas. As I walk South-East, heading toward a cemetery, some verses return: a voice returns to via Appia. It speaks of watching the twilights and the mornings over Rome as acts of Posthistory,

to which I bear witness, for the privilege of recording them from the outer edge of some buried age.

CHAPTER 2

INSCAPE WITH VOICES

1.

Golden leaves gleam, dishevelled against a cloudy sky. There is still something raw and aching about these clouds, although they are vanishing. The entire scene seems covered by a soaked damp veil. Above and below and in the distance and in the forefront, everything is still wet with rain and again it starts shimmering.

Desperate vibrations scrape the silence.

Where lies the spirit of this place? Surely it is rooted within its history, in the shape of these trees and in stories passed on from people to people. It also lies *in the flora and the fauna, in the weather and in the seasons.* In a specific season, at a specific time the spirit of this place unveils to me, as I hear nuances in its sounds and dig into its stories and into its words.

For some time soon after the storm, everything seems quiet. Silence, humid, fruitless. All the sounds seem to be sleeping, or afraid to break out. Then they reappear, tiny needles weaving a fabric of stillness to enfold the arabesques of the songs of hoopoe, chaffinch, turtle dove. Upupa Epops, Fringilla Coelebs, Streptopelia Turtur.

I hear a voice, or it is the wind blowing some muffled verses across the branches?

It isn't of May, this impure air
that darkens the foreigners' dark garden even more...

At twilight, the nightingale will darken this foreigners' dark garden thro' the thick throbbings of her trembling throat.

Enchanted and enchained by the pleasure of a song, soon the cicadas will start buzzing again.

2.

I want to tell you of a song.

It is entitled *Lamento per la morte di Pasolini, Lament for the Death of Pasolini* and it follows the structure of a traditional extra-liturgical religious ballad from Central Italy, the *Orazione di San Donato, Prayer of Saint Donatus*. It was written in December 1975 after Pasolini's death by an Italian singer called Giovanna Marini. It begins like this: *I lost all my strength, I lost my ability.*

I lost all my strength and my ability, at some point about three years ago. Call me a writer of sound. I write of it soaring through the air, leaking into fabrics of words, haunting places and recollections, inhabiting visions and books. At some point about three years ago I felt I'd lost all my strength and my ability; I no longer could see a consistent picture in all I'd done and written over the previous ten years. What had appeared until then like a congruous body of work, crumbled in a myriad scattered pieces that I knew I had to stitch together again.

I lost all my strength and my ability and as I write these pages I go back to my old notebooks. As I read, as I listen and as I write I'm engulfed in an assonant riddle. It hovers between *chi sono? –* in Italian meaning both *who am I?* and *who are they? –* and *chi suono? – whom do I sound? –* voicing the aural universe where my research moves. Many questions, infested by many *who*. These pages swarm with the voices of those questions, and when I say *I* it is in fact *they*: my archive of voices, of words, of sounds, outlining the landscape in which I move. This story is shaped through my collection and my recollections of books, music, sounds, songs; of encounters with books, music, sounds and songs. I inhabit my landscape of readings and of listening moments at times as a guest, at times as a stranger, at times as a parasite, at times as a ghost. I go for a walk around my favourite places of listening, I look for another way of understanding and of stitching those broken pieces together. Until I reach the edge of an abyss.

This is not the outpouring of an autobiographical image: it is an image distorted, reiterated, projected, reinvented and echoed into clusters of words. And not even just one image but clouds of them, attached to the same landscape. It has to do with remembering and returning, today and every other today; with the fixed rhythmic gestures that move my listening, my reading and my writing, where the formulaic quality of certain recurring images outlines the limits within which I can say *I* again.

3.

I spent eleven years in those suburban areas of Rome that imbued Pasolini's work, and as I write I recall the hues in the lights and in the sounds that caress those areas in the spring or early autumn, in the abandoned flame of the morning's burning sun. Desperate vibrations scrape the silence. And I think of the slow pace that invaded the depths of my soul when I truly loved, when I truly wanted to understand.

4.

Giovanna Marini recalls her first meeting with Pasolini in 1958 as a fortuitous encounter, when they shared their love of traditional songs and ballads as possible grounds to found a new language and as keepsakes of oral culture – a culture that back then, in Italy, was still considered unworthy of any consideration. Seventeen years unwind, and in December 1975 Marini sorely paces her way through Pasolini's death in her vernacular ballad constructed by counting the hours: *Lament for the Death of Pasolini*, a folk song echoing a funeral march. In the tight grid of the unravelling hours, her voice appears stronger than ever. The curve of her voice and her delivery of the verses become more and more stringent. They become desperation tightened in a grin, loss sweetened by a moan, edgy gulps mutating into melodic lines. The refrain that gives rhythm to the song is caught between speech and the impossibility of speaking. *He can no longer talk ... My tongue would seek for words*, she sings at the top of her voice, near-shrieking, lacrimosa. And her voice whirls and it bends, outlining a space where it no longer carries any prescriptive or descriptive feel but reaches other heights.

Giovanna Marini's voice was also featured in *Bella Ciao*, a recording of workers', anarchists' and partisans' chants from the 1964 edition of Italy's *Spoleto Festival*, often played by my father when my brother and I were little in the late seventies. We knew the entire record by heart.

We knew all the songs on that record, alongside those in a collection of Alpine chants from World War I, sung a cappella by one of the many traditional choirs from Northern Italy. One song in particular, *The Captain's Testament*, sang of a mutilation of sorts. The captain of a company is mortally wounded and asks his soldiers to cut his body into five pieces: one for Italy, his homeland, one for the company, one for his mother, one for his love and the last one for the mountains, that will cover it with roses and flowers.

My brother and I knew all the songs in *Bella Ciao*, and at the time I was struck by how often one same melody was featured in more than one song, taking on different aspects across songs of abandon and songs of war: not only the well known mutation of *Bella Ciao* from rice weeders' chant to partisan anthem, but the transformation of *Maremma Maremma*, where a girl sings the departure of her lover for the fields in another region, into the lamentation of *Partire partirò, To Leave, I Will Leave* against military conscription.

At the time I was not aware of the significance of the *Bella Ciao* recordings in the resurgence of Italian oral history and folklore. I had no idea of oral culture and its implications in voicing a different tradition, and the whole collection in that record sounded as a texture of mesmerising aural conundrums (many songs were in dialects I'd never heard, and did not understand) and catchy rhythms, kept together by recurring melodies and, of course, voices. Those songs were lifted from their historical time to the time of my listening experience and to the returns of our shared listening experience as a family. Those moments spent in the immediacy of those refrains, the catchiness of those rhymes, the melancholy of songs of departure and the bitterness of songs of abandonment, the sheer joy of sing-along choirs and the naïve innuendos, shaped my sense for listening and my attention to sound a lot more than any structured music lesson – sol-fa, harmony, composition and all – that came afterwards without leaving much of a trace.

On the cover of the *Bella Ciao* vinyl, right under the title spelt in white capital letters, was a large but blurred photograph of what looked like a stage. Four dark silhouettes facing backwards, and four women – three seated, one standing – behind, against a background whose grain was sparse. As a child I was never sure if it was a photograph of the actual show: to me, it looked more like a trial – a heavy, dark atmosphere loomed over the ochre hues of the picture and the stark outlines of the people in it. Between the title and the photograph a short text spoke of certain voices, and of voicing. *Sometimes, from the frescoes and paintings, their faces stare at us. From books though, you hardly ever hear their voices ... Their voices were mistaken with the voices of trees and of yard animals, at the most as the voices of a separate and archaic culture. Today we know they express a world of repressed people in opposition and response.* Seeing that picture and reading those words was an experience veiled with dark undertones; to my childhood ears it felt completely estranged from the songs in the record. Opposition, repression, trial did not resonate with those songs, whereas the sense of darkness conveyed by the text and by the picture stayed within, further deep, only to disclose another layer of understanding many years later.

Many years later I had the chance to read the official press release of the 1964 show. *The songs presented here are examples of the musical expression of the people, caught in their most significant moments: work, leisure, fun, ritual, love, war, social and political protest ... A culture whose characteristics are autonomous from the dominant culture ... In order for* Bella Ciao *to be anything but a folk show, scene props or costumes were removed and the interpreters appear in their everyday clothes, in an abstract dimension made of straw chairs, wooden benches, lights.* What in my childhood I'd read as a trial turned out in fact to be a trial of the cliché idea of folk on one side, and a trial of the very way Italian audiences would look at non-official forms of culture and protest on the other.

Spoleto, Italy, June 1964. The people attending the performance of *Bella Ciao* at the Festival grew restless as they listened to the voices of marble diggers, wheelbarrow carriers, farmers, rice weeders, silk spinners, coalmen, partisans, anarchists resounding on stage, one by one, carving songs out of the mass of their unacknowledged history. Other than that, the festival had featured Ingmar Bergman, Margot Fontaine, Louis Malle, Rudolph Nureyev: none of them could touch so directly and sorely the audience's own pride. The *Bella Ciao* show opened with a preverbal call, taking on the rhythm of an unaccompanied chant by the marble cutters in Carrara, as if pointing at something outside of written tyranny and disclosing its potential in the aural. It softly spread in the hall as Sandra Mantovani suavely vocalised on the rice weeders' version of *Bella Ciao*, soon morphed into the fast-paced partisan version. Later on as Mantovani sung a verse, *We no longer want to die in stables*, a woman shouted, *I own two hundred souls and none of them ever died in a stable!* – so Giovanna Marini recalls. The atmosphere arose into an explosion of voices and dissent. *Boos!* fell down from the gallery. There were the people on stage, their words weighing as much as the explosion of noises around. The audience started laughing, shouting, mocking, whistling and booing, till it all turned into a carnival of infuriating chaos. On stage, they kept singing. Responding with their rhythm to the tension around, making it resonate even stronger.

Toward the end Michele Straniero stood up and started singing *O Gorizia tu sei maledetta, Oh Gorizia You Are Cursed*. He sung this stanza, originally unplanned: *Traitors lords army officers, you have wanted this war / Butchers of sold flesh and spoilers of our youth*. Hell broke loose. *Long live army officers!* followed by *Long live Italy!* choirs arose from the stalls. From the gallery a chair was thrown onto the stalls, while somebody started singing *Bandiera rossa, Red Flag*, the anthem of the Italian Communist Party. In the stalls they sung *Faccetta nera, Little Black Face*, one of the most renowned Fascist army songs. All around, people kept fighting more and more vehemently.

Straniero's rendition of *Oh Gorizia* was particularly controversial because back then in Italy people were only expected to speak (and sing) of war as heroic and patriotic. Many years before, between 9 and 10 August 1916 in Gorizia, North-Eastern Italy, ninety thousand people had lost their lives in one of the bloodiest battles of World War I. Since then, *Oh Gorizia* became one of the anthems of the anarchic and antimilitary tradition; apparently those who were caught singing it were indicted with defeatism and could be shot dead. On the stage in Spoleto in 1964 the rage and discontent of the people was not represented, or made visible as in a flat postcard or nostalgia-laden memento: it was made audible, channelled with all the disruptive, rounded presence of those voices, in the fixity of a now.

The urgency of a situation breaks into a cliché; the explosion of voices from a hidden past clashes with the present tense. It's no longer just the words; it's the voicing of disquiet that matters. The aural matter is the sound of that disquiet. Rumours, lies, noises, buzzes. The history of my country today sounds like a prolonged line of rumours, lies, noises, buzzes. Do I need any more than this? Do I need silence now?

5.

Like the story of the encounter between Pasolini and Marini, like the multiple mutilations in *The Captain's Testament* and like the voices in *Bella Ciao*, my story is a slow accumulation of personal moments of breakthrough in listening, reading, writing.

I draw lines between those moments, I need to shape my understanding.

I need to find my way to the ashes of Gramsci.

6.

The organic adherence by which feeling-passion becomes under-standing, therefore knowledge. These words by Antonio Gramsci hit me today as an epiphany of learning and as foremost keys into listening. To listen is to grasp a deeper sense of place, of self, of stories. In Italian the verb *comprendere, to understand* comes from Latin and means *to embrace.* It is expansive, not normative. It embraces diversity. *Sapere, to know,* comes instead from a verb that means *to have a taste of, to catch a flavour.* And *sentire* in Italian means both *to feel* and *to listen.*

Gramsci's claim for *a shift from knowing to understanding, to feeling, and back, from feeling to understanding, to knowing* encompasses the expanding function of listening: from having a taste of something to embracing it – ultimately, to knowing it. Just like the double shift from light and sound into understanding and backwards, in the slow pace of certain verses written by Pasolini in a collection of poems entitled *Le ceneri di Gramsci, The Ashes of Gramsci,* that I read once *when I truly loved, when / I truly wanted to understand.*

7.

Golden leaves gleam, dishevelled against a cloudy sky. The ashes of Gramsci are kept here, in the Protestant Cemetery in Rome. A recurring place for thinking, and a favoured starting point for walks between cypress trees and along the old Aurelian walls, into the via Appia and the old Roman aqueduct that appears intermittently along its path. There, on a spring day in *an autumnal May*, the daisies and the anemones blossomed white and purple, a silent colourful counterpoint to the soft hiss of the wind-brushed cypress trees. The buzz of cicadas swelled high up and arched above the white and the purple, up above the trees.

Today the sun shines high above my recollections, it lights up the little tinsel vases by the marble slabs while above, on a branch, the far-carrying soft hoo-hoo of a hoopoe calls for more voices: the embellished trill of chaffinch, the gentle purr of turtle dove. All over, the buzz of cicadas throws a maddening, enchanting veil on this cerulean late afternoon. There is still something raw and aching about these clouds although they are vanishing. Rising up toward the sky, the green spiky branches point at my return in the framework of these stones. And yet this place is real and now it is another day, past rusty gates and dark green trees, bushes and moving grass in this flayed and celebrated place, made alive and sounding about fifty years ago by Pasolini's verses. They arrive from a far region of my memory, not from the landscape around me, yet their sound and their pace are as clear to me as the rhythmic tinkle of the little tinsel vases by the marble slabs, stirred by the breeze. How can I make his voice and all the other voices speak, how can I make them audible again?

Golden leaves gleam, dishevelled against a cloudy sky. There is still something raw and aching about these clouds although they are vanishing. I walk away from the Cemetery and direct my steps towards via Appia. Along the Roman aqueduct I recall another voice, slightly familiar though slightly off-centred, arising from some remote region of the mind and from these trees and these walls. It speaks of watching the twilights and the mornings over Rome as acts of Posthistory,

to which I bear witness, for the privilege of recording them from the outer edge of some buried age.

8.

Watching TV on a late afternoon, in a suburban town in Central Italy. A young man with furtive black eyes and a haunted air, wearing a green caped mac and sporting a dishevelled mohawk, moves restlessly on the stage. A young woman appears, dressed up enigmatic in a white tunic and holding a staff. Her style, a nightmarish Art Nouveau: not the sleek lines of Aubrey Beardsley's *Salomé* but the slow, leaden posture of Theda Bara circa *Cleopatra*. In her aspect grace becomes nemesis. The man in the green mac starts to sing – no, it is rather a solemn invocation, vaguely out of tune yet self-assured, just like in a mass choir. The woman stands still. There is an adventurous absolute quality in this setup, it hovers between the imposing and the deranged. It peeks through the man's eyes, that look like two leather buttons. It explodes in every word he sings.

The song is *The Captain's Testament*. Exactly the song by the Alpine choir, featured in my dad's old vinyl. Not exactly that one, so off-centred it sounds. How dare he? He dares. In the delivery of the song the man in the mac carries an awkward air of solemnity, a firm intent. And then the song slowly morphs into a manic, hammering rhythm.

Of course I did not know the term *post punk* at the time. To my teenager ears it was just a manic, hammering rhythm, the skeleton supporting those words: *Curami curami curami, Prendimi in cura da te, Prendimi in cura da te, Cure me Cure me Cure me, Let me be cured by you, Let me be cured by you.* Was it the captain of the soldiers asking to be cured of his wound? Was it the man in a mac pleading to be cured of his malaise? Was it an entire generation of Italian teenagers asking to be cured of Italy? That voice scratched and unmasked my teenager dreams. I suddenly felt alive, awake. It was March 1988, I'd just turned fourteen. A familiar melody had been distorted, and I'd just seen a band called CCCP on TV. Those were not easy years.

Especially today the words of CCCP sound prophetic. They sang of Italy, *province of the empire*. There were rumours, there were lies, there were noises. Buzzes. The sound of those years is a monotonous hum. Rewind, further backwards. Milan, 2 December 1977. The people attending John Cage's performance at Teatro Lirico listened for over three hours to his meticulous and monotonous dissection of Thoreau's diaries that began by omitting phrases, then words, then syllables until there was nothing but sounds. The atmosphere arose into an explosion of voices and dissent. There was Cage, his words weighing as much as the explosion of noises around. The audience started laughing, shouting, mocking, whistling and booing till it all turned into a carnival of infuriating chaos. Cage? He kept reading, responding with poised rhythm to the tension around, making it resonate even stronger. He called his performance *Empty Words*. The urgency of a situation broke into a cliché; the explosion of voices from a hidden past clashed with the present tense. It's no longer just the words, it's the voicing of disquiet that matters. The aural matter is the sound of that disquiet.

Five months later Aldo Moro was murdered by the Red Brigades. I recall the astonishment of our neighbours outside and the deadly silence of my parents when the news broke, followed by all those phone calls as if the sound of daily chatter buzzing itself to oblivion could keep that deathly silence away. Then again there were rumours, there were lies, there were noises, buzzes. Since then, the whole history of my country has been like a prolonged line of rumours, lies, noises, buzzes. Do I need any more than this? Do I need silence now?

9.

Ghosts on via Appia this morning. Twenty degrees, rain and damp. Catacombs of Saint Callixtus, *the archives of the primitive Church*. Ninety acres of land, four levels of subterranean galleries twelve miles long. Half a million tombs. Cemetery of Saint Callixtus, Crypt of Lucina, Cemetery of Saint Soter, Cemetery of Saint Mark, Marcellianus and Damasus, Cemetery of Balbina. Tomb of Cecilia Metella. And when the sun falls down the pine trees I still walk on these stones and there is a humming coming from below the catacombs and these slabs of history. It whispers death along this evening, it breathes in, it breathes out, in, and out, following me chasing me out of this still city of tombs. I keep listening. This still dead city of tombs is chasing me, I walk. Up to this very moment walking, listening, recalling.

I return to via Appia and to those Roman aqueduct arches, and to the mellow suburban countryside on a hot, rainy morning, November 2010. Once it was August, the year 1995, the heat unbearable, the black silhouette of the Cecilia Metella Mausoleum and the maritime pines drawing a silent backdrop to the early evening walk, that you and I had decided to take. We'd spent the whole midsummer day driving around the ring road of Rome, in one direction and backwards, filming – an exorcism against the boredom of that Roman summer and against that whole year, as a double noose holding and hanging that whole year. We'd spent the whole mid-summer day driving around the ring road of Rome, in one direction and backwards, listening – in the extreme sunshine and in the lethargic pace of Roman summers, car windows open wide and music full blast, until the texture of those sounds reached and merged with the melting lights.

I return to via Appia and think of August. Signposts to depots circle like coils on this evening. Your Fiat Punto exhales hundreds of miles. We are going to circle, and circle. You scream, these coils are closing in. You've gone crazy in your rotten daydreaming. You've gone so crazy for your rotten dreaming, it hurts. We circle, enwrapped in this spiral of heat. It arrives as a piercing signal, a ruthless clasp of frequencies pointing right at the essence of rhythm. It arrives as the sound of a new disquieting language; as a rhythmic pattern and oscillation devoid of any reference, other that the push-pull of sound you feel in your body, and the grip of our sonorous now. A bony creature is dancing along the broken structures of audio tracks, built upon the sonic detritus of what once was called techno. Stark on a sensorial plateaux, a thousand needles pierce this sonorous now. Subtle, severe, insidious: here is a plus, here is a minus. A plus, a minus, a minus. Then come the bass sounds, to the earth and up from the earth. Don't tell me these sounds are cold. If something resounds here, it is a shivering body: the body of rhythm exposed in its nerves, in the contractions that keep it alive. It might be mutilated by the cuts of this sonic blade but it is always there, in its presence and denial: a plus, a minus.

I return to via Appia, with you and it is evening. In you Fiat Punto we are listening to *Metri* by Ø, aka Mika Vainio, I think I wrote about this record sometime. Then we park and we walk along the stone-paved street from twilight into night, listening to noises sifted from the sheltered villas. A knot of voices, smells, slivers of light. All the buildings, pines and stones narrated by the daylight have crumbled down into a storyless black. Across the metal bars of gates and the tall brick walls the night is here again. A low hum propagates, made of the same substance of the heat. Our blinded eyes and our deafened ears hope to see a new vision and chase a new melody. I follow the train of my thoughts once more, and the visions of those trains along the tracks down South, to a small town where one of us was born, it has one of the few preserved mythraeums in Italy.

I return to via Appia this evening and I'm lonely. Arthur Conan Doyle set one of his *Tales of Terror* just around here, *The*

New Catacomb. The great Aqueduct of old Rome lay like a monstrous caterpillar across the moonlit landscape, he wrote. This evening the great aqueduct of old Rome in the moonlight doesn't look much like a monster, but as a tamed force. I think again of your tamed silences, the long glances, that way of holding your head in your hand, and your restless longing for a space you will never allow anyone to circumscribe. I'm not sure if it is afternoon or early evening, but I know it was night when you first told me of this sense of waiting, of longing. You are the imminence of a storm of ice, you smell of hunt and blood. Wild dark eyes, every day you lose some glow and you gain some depth and shade. Out of pure will you command your heart to be irregular as nothing ever in your life is regular: not the friends, not the hours, not your lovers or the lives you go through. Now a gentle summer breeze moves through those pine trees, smells of sea salt and resin and cooking and smoke. Tomorrow it's another go, another lap. You crawl. Now I walk back, alone and toward home. I enter the Basilica dei Santi Quattro Coronati and listen to the enclosed nuns as they sing the Vespers. Even the stones are drenched in the void of this confinement. *Spargens sonum,* what is this voice whispering muddled tunes into my ears?

I return to via Appia, and to those Roman aqueduct arches and the mellow suburban countryside, following the steps of Rainer Maria Rilke, Nathaniel Hawthorne, Herman Melville. I am on their traces along the old Roman road, and as I walk I engage with all of them in a series of fictitious interviews.

I ask Rilke of the void he saw in this sky while he walked along these same stones, while these same stones breathed into his verse another type of void, another type of voice. I ask him of how *lieber* rhymes with *Fieber.* I try to anticipate the answer.

I ask Melville of the *solitude and silence* he felt around these Roman walls, in March 1857. Then he felt lost; this morning he is a reminder. To engage in an imaginary interview with Melville is like picturing time in front of me: the time of words when they take time to resound or seep through the mind, the time of thoughts as they take shape into words, the time of actions kept forever inside words. Everything seemed gathered, concluded; it now opens up again and draws a new horizon. It all has to be part of some other yet uncovered landscape.

I ask Hawthorne of an entry in his diary, 23 October 1858. *What now impresses me is the languor of Rome – its nastiness – its weary pavements – its little life pressed down by a weight of death.* Did he know this weight is even heavier today?

Between these unspoken interviews, loaded with memories and echoes, and filigrees of sounds recalled from reading, I do not feel any loss in the absence of my interlocutors. Maybe I just want to be in that silence, in the time of a *recordare*. To record, to recollect.

10.

Now my ears look and long again for Pasolini's voice and verses, across his Roman landscape and across another voice – this time it shrieks, and it's a woman's. It screams and scratches, it puts a spell on me. I met the body of this voice in October 2003, when I interviewed Diamanda Galás in Rome. I asked her to comment on a verse by Pasolini, *Death is not about not being able to communicate, It's about no longer being able to be understood.* She had just released a record, *Defixiones. Will And Testament. Orders From The Dead,* prompted by her long research into the genocides inflicted by the Turks on Anatolian Greeks and Armenians between 1914 and 1923, and into the lost traditions of those people. What does it mean not to be understood? What does it mean to lose one's voice, to be forgotten, to feel a stranger in one's own country? An unforgiving, urgent sequence of chants and litanies is channelled across a tour de force of distortions, loops and manipulated voices. Austere and livid, this is a Sisyphean hell, generated by repetition of words and sentences until they are transformed into incantations. Not by chance, has she often interpreted the classic song by Screamin' Jay Hawkins, *I Put A Spell On You.* Diamanda talks of Pasolini, she embraces those verses as crucial. Understanding, she tells me, is not structural. It has to do with listening to the voice of a people. It is inclusive, and has to be felt. It is born in the body, just like a voice.

Often in her concerts Diamanda interprets a poem by Pasolini, *Supplica a mia madre, Prayer to my Mother: So I must tell you something terrible to know: From within your grace my anguish did grow.*

A poem to the mother – and now I see Orson Welles holding a book entitled *Mamma Roma, Mother Rome.* A poem voicing anguish born out of grace – and the setting is the Flavio Roman aqueduct, and those Roman walls are the same that made Hawthorne feel pressed by anguish born out of beauty. *Desperate vibrations scrape the silence.* Voices in the suburban Roman countryside. I listen *from the outer edge of some buried age* to Orson Welles as he reads, *I am a force from the Past ... I wander ... down via Appia like a dog without a master.*

I listen to the voices in Pasolini's *La ricotta.* I'm displaced as I hear writer Giorgio Bassani lending his voice to Orson Welles who in turn speaks out, on the screen, a poem by Pasolini. Whose voice am I listening to? The one inscribed in Pasolini's poem, the one transposed in Welles' defiant face as he acts the poem on screen, the one conveyed by Bassani's detached pronunciation in the dubbed version of the audio track, or the one reflected in Pasolini's spatial and symbolic filmic arrangement? Pasolini's verses themselves voice a sense of not belonging. As if the sound of the voice in his words could find no place until I, the listener, attach my stories to it and rewrite it into a specific landscape. Recorded, translated, embodied in written text, and back into speech and into a succession of listening moments, that polyphonic voice is not fixed: it exists as it mutates, as it brushes and bangs against the walls of the echo chamber of my mind, inside the numberless metamorphoses of my listening I.

I try to write that voice as if I was recording a number of aural ruminations in spite of myself, encountering myself as a foreigner. The moment of recognition arrives some time later, when I realise how the mutable substance of my listening moments is kept together by the very sense of dissipation that permeates the words to which I give shape after I hear them.

A word in German rescues me: *Stimmung,* a mood, a tonality of being which dictates the tuning of my words modulated according to my inner landscape, and which makes my inner landscape. A piece of writing in response to the experience of listening is like an apparition in this landscape, a flickering hallucination spelt on Sybil's leaves and blown away by a gust. In *La ricotta,* in response to a journalist's stubborn and simplistic questions, Orson Welles reads a poem. He does not reply directly or analytically to the journalist's inquiries but suggests a mood around them, seeping out of himself and the words he reads. In the same manner, as if *from the outer edge of some buried age,* I begin to write.

CHAPTER 3

KNOTS AND SILENCE

1.

Today I returned to via Appia and this evening I return there once again in the pages of a book, *Quer pasticciaccio brutto de via Merulana, That Awful Mess of via Merulana* by Carlo Emilio Gadda. I mirror the recollections of my morning walk against a specific landscape and a specific vision, evoked by the writer when he says the roads and the lights that take further South-East outside of Rome appear as lines streaming out of a crucible of the deep. I reach that part of Gadda's book and read the description of a dawn over Rome, seen from via Appia along the Roman aqueduct.

Gadda describes the sky as it comes back to life across *thin purple strips and remote, clear points of sulphur yellow, and vermillion, strange lacquers, noble reverbs*. Out of a crucible of the deep Rome appears, *a clear proximity of infinite thoughts and buildings*, washed by the wind. The Roman aqueduct ties the architecture of the city, dominated by St. Peter's dome, to the pine trees, the other domes, the towers, and all of it to the *mysterious sources of a dream*.

In Rome, the big boxes of incubating time are heavy with cobwebs. *Rome smothers. Rome smoulders.*

2.

Now I delve into the brooding, leaden pages of another book by Gadda, *La cognizione del dolore*, *Acquainted with Grief*: a far darker literary affair for the writer, in which the pervading loss suffered by the main character merges with his subtly outlined feelings of exile, and of bitterness for a country sunken into Fascism. If a book were to be written about Italy today, it would have to be a continuation of Gadda's Grief. It would not be a choice, any more than breathing is a choice. It would have to be. I know this as I go through each page, imbued with a Cervantic gravitas seeping out of intimately haunted words. Bitterness in a phlegmatic pace is repeatedly shot by satirical bolts: this is the distinctive cadence I hear in these pages, this is their sustained *basso continuo*.

3.

As I continue to write, I am stuck in the impossibility of conveying the distinctive cadence of Gadda's prose for much longer than a fleeting glimpse. Neither am I interested in providing an interpretation of it, nor in reporting biographical anecdotes or a chronology of the work, nor in paraphrasing it. So I project myself to the edge of it, out of these pages and onto those. I find myself trapped in wordlessness, against this writer's abundance of words. The minutiae in Gadda's mixture of dialects, idioms and idiolects, his use of elaborate inflections and technical terms, his obsolete expressions, are hard to hint at in one short paragraph, let alone a page. They remain, still hidden writings to read. What I would choose to retain of this writer's unique texture, and what would be inevitably left out, is the main issue.

This is not the place for me to attempt a report of Gadda's books or a translation, an analysis, a paraphrase. I have no claims to be Gadda's biographer or scholar. I can only point at his books, or dissolve. The writer's story is out there to be discovered, his books are out there to be read. I am so close to those words, I can't do much more than read them again and again. In reverse though, I can let his words point at this story, have them turn yet another page in my book. I need Gadda's accent here, a couple of his glances toward Rome and toward writing, to add another layer to my story.

For four years during World War I Gadda served in a battalion of Alpine soldiers. In his war journals he once wrote of some comrades singing *the song of the pieces*: my personal Siren, *The Captain's Testament*. The voices that first arose in my father's Alpine choirs' vinyl, then across the deranged version of CCCP, are now echoed back into the writer's words.

A dizzying polyphony arises out of the prose of pain of Gadda's war journals, as they implode on the narrating subject;

he would later call them intangible. He never believed in the truth of an absolute past: thirteen years after the end of the war, he wrote an essay entitled *Impossibilità di un diario di guerra, Impossibility of a War Journal*. He denied the faithful quality of his own war chronicle and he emphasised the resonating and shifting qualities of memory, as it scans the surface of every today and falls into its holes, weaving a narrative around gaps and missing pieces.

Gadda looked at the *awful mess* of Rome with the eyes of a sly detective. Forged by a keen recordist of language and its oscillations, his words skate away from any given centre as they move around streets in the urban and suburban landscape. His plurilinguistic stance conjures up a kaleidoscopic world of make-believe and shifting glances: there are no angles in his writing, everything curves and bends just like his via Appia, and the sinewy glance in his description of dawn.

Golden leaves gleam, dishevelled against a cloudy sky. Carlo Emilio Gadda rests in the Protestant Cemetery in Rome. As I walk once more around the Cemetery, the whole city implodes on these pages. Words, sounds and landscape, tied in a knot.

4.

Rome does not speak. Neither the stones, nor the plants have much to say any more.

Rome fell flat on me. Oppressively flat... Silence & loneliness of long streets of blank garden walls... No place where lonely man will feel more lonely than in Rome.

The former entry is from the journals of the Italian poet and writer Cesare Pavese in 1950; the latter is from the journals of Herman Melville nearly a century before, in 1857. It was Pavese who championed the study of Melville in Italy, and it was via Pavese that I became captivated by Melville's world.

We have a talent for silence. Out of a silence loaded with memory, Pavese carved his sentences. I am entranced by the slow pace of his verses, disguised as prose. The same metre of his poems is reflected in his prose: a reading metre, a breathing metre. In 1934 he wrote of how he found his own rhythm: not by looking at the meaning of words, but by repeatedly muttering a chant across them, an emphatic cadence that had been with him since he was little and that he would attach to each novel or text he read. He called such method *the rhythm of his fantasising*: he let his voice find its way through his inner breathing cadence first, before any meaning.

A firm believer in stories subsumed and disclosed within landscape, Pavese wrote of a *pictorial commotion* as the primary force that moved his words. *At the ground of this fantasy of mine lies a pictorial commotion ... I had discovered the* image *... This image was, obscurely, the story itself.* Pasolini too once wrote of a pictorial commotion, he called it *a figurative fulguration.* He also wrote of tradition, reinvented every time by his narrating voice: a *force of the past* that records images *from the outer edge of some buried age.* His words unwittingly echo Pavese's, *to have a tradition is less than* *nothing, it is only by looking for it that you can experience it* – a sentence that appeared in the writer's introduction to his 1941 Italian translation of *Moby-Dick*.

Pavese spent a week in Rome between 30 December 1949 and 6 January 1950, a few months before his suicide. On New Year's Day he wrote in his journal, *Rome does not speak. Neither the stones, nor the plants have much to say any more.* As I walk across the stone-paved streets and I look at these buildings, I think of this city that has not much to say any more.

Melville spent three weeks and a half in Rome in the early spring of 1857, and recorded those days in his journal.

28 February. Silence & loneliness of long streets of blank garden walls.

1 March. The Porta Maggiore. Finest ancient gate in Rome. Baker's tomb. Aqueducts. Mass of brick. To the Basilica of St. John Lateran. Loneliness of the spot by Giovanni Gate height looking down from walls...

Like an epitaph, Melville's last words in the eternal city:

Walk along the walls outside. Solitude & silence. Passing gates walled up. Perfect hush of all things.

5.

Melville's mapping of Rome takes the shape of a clash between crumbling grandeur and feelings of isolation. His meanderings around the city find a centre of gravity in a familiar ground, where golden leaves gleam, dishevelled against a cloudy sky:

> 27 February. After much trouble & some travel without a guide manage to get to Protestant Burial Ground & pyramid of Cestius under walls. Read Keats' epitaph. Separated from the adjacent ground by trench. Shelley in other ground. Plain stone.

Shelley said the idea of being buried in the Protestant Cemetery in Rome might make one fall in love with death. And John Keats on his deathbed, hearing that daisies and anemones grew wild on the graves under the cypress trees in the Cemetery, said he could already feel the flowers growing over him.

The ashes of Gramsci are also kept here. The Cemetery used to be one of my recurring places for thinking, and a favoured starting point for walks between cypress trees and along the old Aurelian walls, into the via Appia and the old Roman aqueduct that appears intermittently along its path. There, on a spring day in *an autumnal May*, the daisies and the anemones blossomed white and purple. Around, the buzz of cicadas swelled high up, and arched above the white and the purple, up above the wearily agitated cypress trees.

Today the sun shines high above my recollection, it lights up the little tinsel vases by the marble slabs while above, on a branch, the far-carrying soft hoo-hoo of a hoopoe calls for more voices. There is still something raw and aching about these clouds although they are vanishing. Rising up toward the sky, these green spiky branches point at my return in the framework of these stones. And yet this place is real, and again it is an autumnal spring, behind rusty gates and dark green trees, bushes and moving grass in this flayed and celebrated place, made alive and sounding about fifty years ago by Pasolini.

Golden leaves gleam, dishevelled against a cloudy sky. There is still something raw and aching about these clouds although they are vanishing. I recall another voice, slightly familiar though slightly off-centred, arising from some remote region of the mind and from these trees and these walls: *And we dead too, with you, in the humid garden.* This *humid garden* in the Protestant Cemetery is the initial setting for Pasolini's *The Ashes of Gramsci.* Written in 1954 and published the following year, the poem was a song of conflict torn between romantic drive and social engagement. Alone in the Cemetery, Pasolini engages in a silent dialogue with Gramsci, with Shelley, with himself and his country: he creates imaginary conversations within the borders of his inner landscape. The poem is written in *terza rima,* just like Dante's *Divine Comedy*: the horizon of Pasolini's inner landscape. It is not the outpouring of an autobiographical mirror image: it is this image distorted, reiterated, projected, reinvented and echoed into clusters of words. It does not have to do with one image, but with a cloud of them. It has to do with remembering and returning rather than creating. It has to do with the fixed rhythmic gestures that move the poet's reading and his writing, where the regularity of the *terza rima* and the formulaic quality of certain recurring images protect the discourse from the overflow of passion, and outline the limits within which he can say *I* again. Now there's some feeling. Now there's some hearing. Now there's some understanding:

> I understand, silent in the wind's soaked
> humming, here where Rome is silent
> . . . .

CHAPTER 4

THE AMBIGUITIES: FIVE BLANK PAGES, *PIERRE*, THE BOOK

*

Early one morning in the middle of August 2007 I walked from the Protestant Cemetery to the Porta Portese street market. On a stall I found an Italian translation of *Pierre* by Melville, the best fifteen Euro I could have spent: I'd been obsessed with that book for a few years and to see it reappear as a second-hand volume on a stall stirred me to a certain degree of excitement.

I look again at the book today. It isn't in great condition; it was printed in 1942, the vermilion hardcover isn't too battered but the pages are very yellow and thin, and the glue in the spine has almost completely gone.

Five pages in the book are blank: the imprints of the letter-press are there, but the ink is missing. I remember when I first found it out: to see five blank pages in the book where Melville places writing dangerously on its edges, and where the question of writing appears as the unresolved clash between the writing of nothing and a creative force in spite of all, seemed too tempting a hand stretched out of chance.

I knew back then, some day I would fill those blank pages with words.

+

The five blank pages in my second-hand Italian copy of *Pierre* have stayed blank all these years. Today I've embraced the idea of copying, in each of those empty pages, excerpts from the original English book, alongside thoughts and words I've been exploring and weaving together in my own pages.

So far I have considered the following five possibilities:

A.

On the unstable equilibrium between writing as creation and writing as end

Pierre is a book shaped around the conflict between the impossibility of conveying any profundity in writing, and the tension to write out of a profound drive nonetheless. It subtitle, *The Ambiguities*, marks such a condition. In the second half of the story – although reducing any work by Melville to a *story* does not pay justice to the spin-offs, digressions, points of stillness and repetition which make each one of his books – the narrator engages in a meditation on the eponymous character, caught as he attempts to write *some shallow nothing of a novel:*

> Here surely is a wonderful stillness of eight hours and a half, repeated day after day. In the heart of such silence, surely something is at work. Is it creation, or destruction? Builds Pierre the noble world of a new book? or does the Pale Haggardness unbuild the lungs and the life in him? ... Is there then all this work to one book, which shall be read in a very few hours; and, far more frequently, utterly skipped in one second, and which, in the end, whatever it be, must undoubtedly go to the worms? ... Not so, that which now absorbs the time and the life of Pierre, is not the book, but the primitive elementalizing of the strange stuff, which in the act of attempting that book, has upheaved and upgushed in his soul. Two books are being writ, of which the worlds shall only see one, and that the bungled one. The larger book, and the infinitely better, is for Pierre's own private shelf. That it is, whose unfathomable cravings drink his blood, the other only demands his ink. But circumstances have so decreed, that the one can not be composed on the paper, but only as the other is writ down in his soul. And the one of the soul is elephantinely sluggish, and will not budge at a breath. Thus Pierre is

fastened by two leeches; – how then can the life of Pierre last? Lo! he is fitting himself for the highest life, by thinning his blood and collapsing his heart. He is learning how to live, by rehearsing the part of death.

B.

On reading and knots of reference

Reading for Melville can lead to discovering *darker threads* infiltrated by the writer in the plot. It happened in *Moby-Dick* with *The Town-Ho's Story* told by Ishmael, in which he interweaved *in its proper place the darker thread with the story as publicly narrated on the ship.* Both writer and reader are woven into the fabric of the story. The *infinite entanglements of all social things, which forbid that one thread should fly the general fabric, on some lines of duty, without tearing itself and tearing others,* make it impossible for a writer to produce a text disentangled.

I once read a letter of Melville to Hawthorne, in which he referred to his books as *botches: June 1951. What I feel most moved to write, that is banned, — it will not pay. Yet, altogether, write the other way I cannot. So the product is a final hash, and all my books are botches.*

Something in Melville's words reminds me of Gadda, who also once wrote of knots: *Each one of us appears to me as a botch, or a knot, or a tangle, of physical and metaphysical relationships.*

C.

On layers

I read again *Pierre*'s words on the riddle between surface and depth. I think of these layers, of the quest for profundity as it is frustrated and reinstated on yet another surface, through yet another layer. It doesn't have to do with a final discovery, but with the movements and the transformations that let the traces of each profound experience emerge across words on the surface of every now. I think of my walks and falls and I think of writing-as-landscape and its porous substance.

Far as any geologist has yet gone down in the world, it is found to consist of nothing but surface stratified on surface. To its axis, the world being nothing but superinduced superficies. By vast pains we mine into the pyramid; by horrible gropings we come to the central room; with joy we espy the sarcophagus; but we lift the lid – and no body is there! – appallingly vacant as vast is the soul of a man! ... For the more and the more that he wrote, and the deeper and the deeper that he dived, Pierre saw the everlasting elusiveness of Truth, the universal lurking insincerity of even the greatest and purest written thoughts. Like knavish cards, the leaves of all great books were covertly packed. He was but packing one set the more; and that a very poor jaded set and pack indeed.

D.

On artifice

All in *Pierre* is artificial. As I read I'm caught in a net of words that deliberately points at the book's fictitious nature. It appears right from the beginning, where the description of the landscape of Saddle Meadows is too pastoral to be believed, too perfect to be credible; where in each dialogue the characters continually point at the artificiality of their tone.

I think of an Italian writer called Giorgio Manganelli and of one of his books entitled *Interviste impossibili, Impossible Interviews,* in which the web of words makes up a realm of surfaces and slippery planes dissolving into a void. Often Manganelli referred to a notion of *literature as lie;* and Melville's Pierre at some point says, *the truest book in the world is a lie.* I read the imaginary interview that Manganelli staged with Leopoldo Fregoli, the famous Italian quick-change artist from the turn of the last century: *Inside human beings, inside beasts and inside things, there is a shiver of horror: they are nothing, and they know it.*

I juxtapose these words with Melville's own literary experiment in quick-change: the relay dialogues of *The Confidence-Man.* Published in 1957, it was the last novel he wrote before his turn to poetry; it staged the ongoing dialogue, across several transformations, of the same shifting character as he took on different aspects: *But if the acutest sage be often at his wit's end to understand living character, shall those who are not sages expect to run and read character in those mere phantoms which flit along a page, like shadows along a wall?*

The Confidence-Man is ultimately an experiment with *character,* intended both as persona and as letter. I think of Manganelli/Fregoli's nothing and ever-shifting character against Melville/Confidence-Man's convoluted prose of non-transparency, and its direct hint at the signs of writing against an underlying void: *You would have thought he spoke less to mere auditors than to an invisible amanuensis; seemed talking for the press; very impressive way with him indeed. And I, having an equally impressible memory, think that, upon a pinch, I can render you the judge upon the colonel almost word for word.*

E.

On reading.

Pierre is the story of a reader who attempts to become a writer. I rewrite and repeat, then stare at the following words *ad libitum*:

> How swiftly and how wonderfully, he reads all the obscurest and most obliterate inscriptions he finds in his memory; yea, and rummages himself all over, for still hidden writings to read.

For still hidden writings to read, for still hidden writings
  to read.

Part 11

CHAPTER 5

A SKY HEAVY WITH CLOUDS

FROM THE NOTEBOOKS ON READING

5.

10 April 2008.

I walked in Rome on stone-paved streets today, and I thought of how the Italian poet and writer Cesare Pavese was pervaded by a sense of ending as he walked along these same streets. Stillness and a silence of stone seep through his words. *Rome does not speak,* he wrote in his journals in 1950. The same sense of ending and the same deadly silence permeate Pavese's collection of poems *La terra e la morte, Earth and Death,* written during his first stay in Rome in 1945, in which the features of a woman and the sense of void and stillness are made of the same substance as the landscape. Then I thought of an old sailor described by Herman Melville in the latter part of his life – after all, it was because of Pavese's Italian translation of *Moby-Dick* that I became captivated by the world of the American writer. The sailor appeared in one of the very last known pieces of writing by Melville, *Daniel Orme* – the story of an end and the story of a move from coast to inner land – in which the death of the main character, a retired sailor, is ingrained in the description of the landscape and in the horizon, and earth is death because it is not sea.

Coming home after my walk I juxtaposed Pavese's verses in *Earth and Death* with Melville's Daniel Orme, in the attempt to transform a pictorial commotion into a story, from inscape to edge to abyss.

4.

11 April 2008

The character in Pavese's poem always comes from the sea, speaks with its hoarse voice, always has secret eyes, *And a low forehead, like / A sky heavy with clouds.* Daniel Orme's eye ... *was a tutoring and deterring one. ... His features were large, strong, cast as in iron; but the effect of a cartridge explosion had peppered all below the eyes with dense dottings of black-blue. ... his tanned brow showed like October's tawny moon revealed in crescent above an ominous cloud.*

In Pavese's words *Death begins again. / Savage, unknown creature, you are reborn from the sea.* Melville's *Orme was discovered alone and dead on a height overlooking the seaward sweep of the great haven to whose shore, in his retirement from sea, he had moored. ... He faced the outlet to the ocean. The eyes were open, still containing in death the vital glance fixed on the hazy waters and the dim-seen sails coming and going or at an anchor near by.*

3.

11 April 2011.

I read again an essay by Carlo Emilio Gadda, published in 1950 and entitled *Come lavoro, How I Work.*

Each one of us appears to me like a botch, or a knot, or a tangle, of physical and metaphysical relationships ... It is not given to me to state anything. The natural limpidity of our innermost, truest statement, is diverted and soiled since the beginning. An unknown hand, as of iron, superimposes on our child-hand, it holds the quill without being entitled to: it takes it to abstinent letters and pages, and nearly to the saving lies.

2.

12 April 2011.

I compare Gadda's *saving lies,* leading the writing hand, to Manganelli's notion of *literature as lie,* outlined by him in the sixties in a number of literary reviews, articles and short essays, later collected as a book.

Whereas in Gadda's books verbal copiousness takes on the inclusive shape of a knot, in Manganelli's prose lexical accumulation crumbles down in a huge, resonating space beneath the surfaces of words. *The literary object is dark, dense, plump, opaque, crammed with casual folds, it constantly mutates its lines of break, it is a silent plot of sounding words.* He stigmatises any attempt at making sense of writing, and urges instead to pay attention to what he calls *the subtle noise of prose*: the ineffable, persistent quality arising out of the texture and the rhythm of words, that remains after reading certain novels even if one forgets the names of their characters.

Manganelli recurs to two Latin words to frame his notion of *literature as lie* as it unfolds in his writing: *inventio* and *artificium, invention* and *artifice.* The former comes from the verb *invenio* and denotes an operation of finding by means of memory. Literature appears as a subtly sounding construction, built from the past: it creates *nothing new,* but a rearrangement of pre-existing elements fashioned into a new shape by recalling and arranging them in the present tense. *Artificium* in turn denotes art, profession; skill, ability; system; artifice, trick. Literature is enveloped by its shadows and by the spell of rhetoric. It is not only a lie but also a vice, a trick supporting an anti-historical stance. Manganelli says his task as a writer is not to create, but to classify *written creatures* and their abundance of words, hence to create a system of evoking and channelling what is already there: still, hidden writings to read.

1.

16 April 2011.

In a short essay entitled *Così noti così clandestini, So Known So Clandestine* Manganelli proposes to read books by known authors leaving aside any knowledge of their status, dismissing any scholarly tradition that supports the act of reading. He calls for closeness to words as they are unfolded: each new reading moment exists as a return and a discovery at once. The space of reading appears like a hunting scene, where the reader is familiar with the landscape yet cannot always predict what might happen on any return: an accident, a lucky chance, a happy discovery, an assault.

In this hunting scene I look for still hidden writings to read, in this hunt I look at still hidden writings to read, in the hunt I might even end up with nothing special.

What is special about this nothing is how I get there, and what I make of the experience of reading every time I return. Every time haunted or charged by the past, every time informed by the new: a progression of moments of awareness amassed into each now with all its load of then's.

To read and read again. To recognise and discover more, until I realise how immediate and how singular each reading experience is. Like when I travel back to a landscape known and surprising at once, thrilled at the thought of returning and concerned at the thought of finding myself a stranger in what once was familiar. To read again consolidates a sense of *being there* as I write.

Following Manganelli's argument, reading appears to be like a forgotten currency which can be used to buy the most precious, priceless nothing: an ever-changing, ever-familiar experience. I go through or skip away from lines I believed I knew by heart; I read what I thought I'd misread, I read again what I thought I'd read, I find myself distracted in points that once took all my attention, I rejoice again at certain turns and bends of phrase. Reading is the drive to breathe a singular voice into still words, to find an individual path into their texture and substance, to search for resonant inflections. It happens before categories, just like listening. In the same manner as the off-centred chanting of CCCP did not sound to my teenager ears as *post punk* but as a manic hammering rhythm, in the same manner as hearing the songs in *Bella Ciao* as a child before I knew what they meant actually allowed me to build *my* meaning through them.

I return to words as if in a secret place, real as I go through it, as I make it anew every other today and as I move along its edges. I arrange in the same landscape the words of Pasolini and Melville, of Gadda and Ethel B., I fall across them.

CHAPTER 6

FROM THE OUTER EDGE OF SOME

BURIED AGE

FROM THE NOTEBOOKS ON WRITING

SOUND

10.

5 February 2011.

A piece of writing in response to the experience of listening is like an apparition in a landscape, a flickering hallucination spelt on Sybil's leaves and blown away by a gust.

In Pasolini's film *La ricotta*, in response to a journalist's simplistic questions, Orson Welles reads a poem. He does not reply directly or analytically to the journalist's inquiries but suggests a mood around them, seeping out of the words he reads. In the same manner, as if *from the outer edge of some buried age*, I begin to write.

+

I begin to think of Writing Sound as I recall a short text by Robert Walser, published in 1902 and entitled *Music*. At some point he says, *there's something missing when I don't hear music, and when I do, then there's really something missing. That's the best I can say about music.* I wish to explore this space, delineated by *really something missing* as the best that can be said about music. I wish my thoughts to exist right at the heart of Walser's hopelessness for an encounter between music and words. And I wish to look at how writing sound fills a space apparently void, yet loaded;

empty, but only just so. Music and sounds still resonate there, they can be sensed seeping through the words that speak the absence – or shall I say, that inscribe the absence?

Sound exists in Walser's words *in absentia*, but it also exists in the actuality of its being written. The sense of missing calls for words: they crowd up against an outline of emptiness, swarm inside it, redefine and inhabit the space left by sound.

I think of this space as a landscape in perpetual transformation – occupied by sounds, left by them, filled in by words across recollections or anticipations, and over again. I look at the many ways of returning to and inhabiting this ever-changing, ever-familiar landscape as it is written. It is impossible to predict what might happen on any return: an accident, a happy discovery, a moment of contemplation, a fall. Or even nothing special. What is special about this nothing is its very precarious yet loaded quality, that I sense in my experience of being there, *in listening*, and not being there any longer, *in writing* – every time charged by the past, every time detached from it and informed by the new: a progression of moments of awareness, amassed into the now with all its load of then's. Such a condition of estrangement from sounds does not call for unattainable wholeness, for absolute frameworks and legitimate ways of understanding, but rather for a syncretic, personal rearrangement of one's array of the memories that shape each listening moment today. Such condition of estrangement from sound does not call for a complete, discursive space but for the making and the unmaking of memories in a contingent present singular.

As I listen to sounds and then set out to write, I become more and more aware of my distance from them. My words cannot capture them: they let them go astray, dissolve. Instead, my words inscribe sounds with their own presence; they answer the enigma of sounds with yet another enigma.

I read David Toop's words in *Sinister Resonance: If we expect sound merely to give, or to invade, just like the earth digger on the building site or the bass drum, then we miss the other side. Better we should think of sound as an ear, a mirror, a resonant echo, a carrier, a shell.* What is the question that I whisper in that ear? What do I see appearing in the mirror of listening? What do I ask of sound? What echoes out of sound as I listen?

I think of writing as *the other side* of sound. Instead of looking for answers it echoes questions with questions, riddles with riddles, it adds complexity to complexity. Writing sound traces the shifting in the tuning of my words, of my questions, of sounds drifting.

When I listen and then I write, the point is in sustaining a double movement of estrangement from, and recognition of sounds, which does not call for synaesthesia but for a cohabitation of worlds. A frayed pattern of words envelops each new page, together with the experience that originated it. The movement of these words is one of difference and inclusion: although it exists in another medium it keeps very close to the materials that prompted it, to how they are, how they sound, how they feel.

I think of Writing Sound as I read *Philosophy of Landscape*, a text published by Georg Simmel in 1913. He shows how landscape perceived as a unity is in fact the result of an activity of the human gaze – of the artistic gaze in particular – that fills in a number of discreet signals and constructs *a* landscape, every time anew. Simmel uses the German word *Stimmung* meaning *atmosphere, mood,* and *tuning.* For him, mood, atmosphere and tuning do not portray a landscape as a whole still entity but *make* it over and over, across fluctuations and nuances that register how we situate ourselves in it: a construction that does not have to do with permanence, but exists and changes culturally and historically. I would like to expand this notion of *Stimmung* from looking to writing, as an activity shaped by the impermanence of sounds and by how we tune in them. I then think of writing sound as a landscape insisted upon and modified by personal instances of listening, and of remembering listening; a collection and a recollection of places, mixed with invention but true to the score drawn by each singular experience.

I think of Writing Sound as the trace of the experience that makes it. It conveys the sense of shaping, step by step along the journey of the listening and the writing *I*, words into places at once familiar and strange.

9.

16 December 2004. Between this unspoken interview, loaded with memories and echoes, and filigrees of sounds recalled from hearing, I did not feel any loss in the silence of my interviewee. Maybe I just wanted to be in that silence.

22 April 2011.

I first wrote these sentences after an unspoken interview I did a few years ago: not an imaginary one with the missing characters of Melville, Hawthorne and Rilke but one that took place in silence, or apparently so.

On a winter afternoon in 2004 I sat in the lounge of Mika Vainio's house in Berlin. For about an hour he played a number of vinyl records from his collection. We barely said a word.

We listened. As Mika put each vinyl back in its sleeve, and proceeded to placing the next on the record player, I engaged in a wordless conversation with the space and the sounds, the melodies and the words, the signals and the frequencies all around. I drew thoughts and words out of the aural cloud hovering around me. I caught clues.

Today I know: that afternoon a special form of interview took place. The substance of listening disclosed as it took over the space of words. The pacing of melodies and sounds, the stories I would imagine within that aural construction were more than enough for me to write about. Now I recall that space, I linger on its haunting complexity as I pick up a trail of clues dropped by Mika across a chain of listening moments. Graeme Revell's *Insect Musicians*. An unknown rockabilly voice honking out of a heavy disc of black shellac. A more-than-black shrieking voice layered upon time-imploding percussions. John Cage's *Fontana Mix*. The score of John Cage's *Fontana Mix*.

When I inadvertently dropped on the floor the glass of wine I was drinking I expected a crash but there was a carpet, and the fall only resulted in a muffled sound. After that accident, Revell's insects sounded even more eerie, their frequencies even more pointy. It hits me now, how the focus of that afternoon was as much in the specific tracks or even snippets of sounds and graphic scores as in the listening experience as a whole, while Mika stitched together the sequence of his records, and I as a listener would weave a second layer of reference across them.

Mika's unsettled sounds had appeared many years before. 1994. It arrives as a piercing signal, a ruthless clasp of frequencies pointing right at the essence of rhythm. It arrives as the sound of a new disquieting language; as a rhythmic pattern and oscillation devoid of any reference, other that the push-pull of sound felt in the body, and the grip of a sonorous now. A bony creature dances along the broken structures of audio tracks, built upon the sonic detritus of what once was called techno. A record, *Metri*, and its rhythm reduced to the prime causes of its existence: the physical perception of movement, the mental perception of rhythmic structure. Between the two a mutual and seamless transfer takes place, in which rhythm and the idea of rhythm are transformed in a hybrid figure, which exists in the brain and reaches out into the body. Stark on a sensorial plateaux, a thousand needles pierce this sonic now. Subtle, severe, insidious: here is a plus, here is a minus. A plus, a minus, a minus. Then come the bass sounds, to the earth and up from the earth. If something resounds here, it is a shivering body: the body of rhythm exposed in its nerves, in the contractions that keep it alive. It might be mutilated by the cuts of this sonic blade but it is always there, in its presence and its denial: a plus, a minus.

Today I recall Mika's music as a primordial blackness. The first time I heard a DJ set by him was in 2001. I remember broken glass and rusty window frames in the small office room of an otherwise vast abandoned warehouse in Milan, on the edge of an evening. The light in my recollections today appears like a grainy patina. I only recall the sounds at the beginning of that DJ set, then nothing but the stupor in the faces of the audience. A black tabula rasa stayed within, after the initial piercing cries: an unbearable volume blasted out the excruciating whip of an otherworldly voice. Later Mika told me it was Keiji Haino, and only many years later I got hold of a copy of that record, *A Challenge to Fate*, punctuated by lashings of muffled howls, erasing any type of rhythmic tease and pointing at an absolute magmatic noise, the all-pervading black, synonym of fall, symbol of the seduction of the fall. For many years and still today, that moment evoked the essence of Mika's movements into sound: pointing at that black. And then I just wanted to be in silence.

8.

20 August 2010.

Do I need silence now? Where do I read silence? How do I write silence?

I think of Writing Sound as I read *A King Listens* by Italo Calvino, a short story published posthumously in 1986 as part of an unfinished collection dedicated to the five senses. It is the story of a king who lives alone in a constant state of surveillance, capturing every acoustic signal in his palace as a sign of a plot against himself and his status. Writing of listening as an isolated act, Calvino points right at the heart of the paradox of writing sound. I would like to look more closely at the very distinctive voice in this story.

Throughout his text Calvino uses the second person, a powerful singular *you*, and by doing so the reader is placed constantly on the edge: that *you* is highly ambiguous and one is never sure if it's the writer addressing the king who listens, the king's mind addressing the listening king, the writer addressing the reader-as-king as he or she listens, Calvino using his text as a mirror to reflect his words unto us, the readers.

Alone, the king listening to the silence around him and in turn, the reader reading and the writer writing the story and its threatening silence, become the figure of a solipsistic exercise verging into the buzz of paranoia. The king's palace is but an ear. He sits lonely on top of his throne. Around, silence swarms with voices as he listens to *time as it goes by* and its *sonorous numbers*. Inside, silence is not the absence of signal, but the absence of a space articulated outside of the experience of listening as such. In one of his moments of doubt the king/narrator wonders, *Is there a story that links one noise to another?*. Listening then needs to be articulated, attached to something outside of itself, otherwise it falls into a status of isolation and self-referentiality. The *you singular* in Calvino's story signifies the hesitancy of the narrator between the elusiveness of the aural dimension as such, and the necessity to extend it across words.

At last the king goes out of his palace and his ear is caught by a melody. He hears a woman singing and he no longer pays attention to the plotting of his lonely mind. He reaches out and sings a duet with her: his experience of listening now takes place in an articulated, rounded dimension. The sense of precariousness, the hovering site of the listener represented by the lonely king and by that ambiguous *you*, slippery and placeless, is resolved by Calvino by shaping the listening experience of a singular you in a story that reaches out to many I's, she's and he's.

But this is not to say that they reply.

+

23 August 2010.

Do you think in the box... or do you think in your head?, Tarwater asks his uncle Rayber in Flannery O'Connor's book *The Violent Bear It Away*. The three main characters in the novel are all deaf, in some way or another. Bishop, the *dim-witted child*: deaf by birth. Rayber, his father: deaf by accident. He uses a hearing aid and his entire character is a study into degrees of self-imposed silence and distance in perception. Tarwater, the antihero: not literally deaf, but deaf to anything that happens around him except for his intent.

A lot of this novel is shaped on mishearing, on assuming to hear or pretending not to, on hearing voices from hidden recesses of one's own mind, on placing and displacing voices, on the calling of the voice of what is assumed and forced to be religion. Entire scenes are described by means of aural perception and of aural distance; each sounding shade overwhelms the vision and the space it inhabits, it is absorbed in the wholeness of the narration. *The machine made the sound seem to come from inside him as if something in him were tearing itself free.*

+

25 August 2010.

Neither Calvino nor O'Connor were specifically concerned with describing sound or moments of listening as self-contained experiences: the aural dimension, as it is written, exists within the complexity of their stories, where *sound* is neither an absolute nor a central category. It is encompassed in their ways of shaping their words, to carry *all those concrete details of life that make actual the mystery of our position on earth* as writers, as O'Connor would have it. To be a writer you must know how to look at the world around you, and how to listen. *The fiction writer begins where human perception begins. He appeals to the senses ... Some people have the notion that you read the story and then climb out of it into the meaning, but for the fiction writer himself the whole story is the meaning, because it is an experience, not an abstraction.*

I think of Writing Sound as the mapping of the experience that drives it, in constant motion between feeling, knowing, understanding: to shape, report or recall an act of listening in words is an inclusive gesture, not an abstraction. It is driven by a way of seeing and telling the world, ingrained within words that necessarily branch out of the aural dimension as such to reach characters and places and memories, woven again and again into the now.

7.

27 April 2011.

The first time I visited the Protestant Cemetery in Rome, it was shut.

In typical Italian style somebody had decided, without announcing it, that it would only be open on a restricted schedule. It was the spring of I no longer remember which year of the nineties.

After a long period of anticipation – to visit the tombs of adored poets Keats and Shelley! – I had to get back in my car and drive back home, disappointed. The only thing that made up for my missed visit was a book, which I'd bought on the same day. It was entitled *The Ashes of Gramsci*, it was a collection of poems written by Pier Paolo Pasolini in the fifties, and it allowed me to see and hear the Protestant Cemetery for the first time, although in words: in *terza rima* verses to be precise, chosen by Pasolini to give rhythm to his silent dialogue with Gramsci and with Shelley, in the setting of the Cemetery on *an autumnal May*.

That evening my visit to the Cemetery took the form of a Proustian anticipation. Instead of actually being there, I fashioned my visit upon the words of Pasolini. I imagined to raise my eyes and see the *foam-streaked sky*; I could hear the sound of faded hammers from the nearby workshops in Testaccio; as a silent witness, I could hear Pasolini's imaginary conversation with the founder of the Italian Communist Party and with the Romantic poet, while he unravelled his struggle between social engagement and romantic tension; I could picture in my mind the *waxen light* curdle in the twilit neighbourhood and hear the *dim hum* of life encompassed in those verses; I could nearly feel the soft breeze, *dying with shivers of storms,* graze my face.

Pasolini's verses are now ingrained in my experience of the place and every time I return there I can't prevent myself from hearing them, in the same manner as I couldn't prevent myself today, on returning to the Cemetery, from hearing the songs of hoopoe and chaffinch. I once learned those verses by heart, I hear them any time I return.

By heart I hear.

+

28 April 2011.

I go back to my copy of *The Ashes of Gramsci*. *This foreigners' dark garden, desperate vibrations scrape the silence* and *silent, humid, fruitless* are verses I underlined on every subsequent visit to the Protestant Cemetery, accompanied by that book. On its back pages I once made a note of the assonant line, *Thro' the thick throbbings of her trembling throat*, recalled from another poem, *The Nightingale* by Algernon Charles Swinburne. I made a note of it the first time I heard a nightingale, on exiting the Cemetery early one evening. I liked the way the song of the bird merged with the buzz of cicadas – a sound that fills many summer days and evenings in Rome. I then thought of the myth of the birth of cicadas, narrated by Plato in *Phaedrus*: of men who existed before the Muses, and who died from the pleasure of listening to their song. They were eventually transformed into cicadas, and granted to sing in eternity. I have always been inclined to draw a parallel between this myth and the delirious quality of listening: the disclosure of sound within the exhilarating experience of listening, and within every account of such experience in words.

As I write of my repeated listening moments in the Protestant Cemetery through the filter of Pasolini's verses and of my memories, what I outline cannot be but a layered construction of all the thoughts and words and sounds that have been with me on every visit through the years, and that hit my every return – a syncretism of my every now, with its load of then's amassed on it.

There is no claim for authenticity or immediacy in my picture of the Cemetery. It doesn't matter what is real and what is fake in its repeating patterns. I shift the glance and the ear to its texture, woven in such a hybrid operation. Rather than interrogating the provenance and aim of this scene, I'd lose myself in its spinning vortex of recalled, reinvented and revisited images, sounds and words. I no longer know what was real and what I imagined, what I heard and what I made myself believe I was hearing. Today I construct a place, I channel a presence as a frayed palimpsest of notated experiences, anticipations, recollections.

+

29 April 2011.

An attempt to picture the Cemetery.

Golden leaves gleam, dishevelled against a cloudy sky. There is still something raw and aching about these clouds, although they are vanishing. The entire scene seems covered by a soaked damp veil. Above and below and in the distance and in the forefront, everything is still wet with rain, but again it starts shimmering. Golden leaves gleam, dishevelled against a cloudy sky. Desperate vibrations scrape the silence. Where lies the spirit of this place? Surely it is rooted within its history, in the shape of these trees, and in stories passed on from people to people. It also lies *in the flora and the fauna, in the weather, and in the seasons.* In a specific season, at a specific time, the spirit of this place unveils to me, as I hear and uncover nuances in its sounds and dig into its stories and into the words inscribed in it. Desperate vibrations against a cerulean cloudy sky. For some time, soon after the storm, everything seems quiet. Silence, humid, fruitless. All the sounds seem to be sleeping, or afraid to break out. Then they reappear: the rhythmic tinkle of the little tinsel vases by the marble slabs, stirred by the breeze, as tiny needles weaving a fabric of stillness, now open to the arabesques of the song of hoopoe, chaffinch, turtle dove. Upupa Epops, Fringilla Coelebs,

Streptopelia turtur. I can hear a voice, or it is the wind blowing muffled verses across the branches? It isn't of May, this impure air that darkens the foreigners' dark garden even more... At twilight, the nightingale will darken this foreigners' dark garden, thro' the thick throbbings of her trembling throat. Golden leaves gleam, dishevelled against a cloudy sky. Enchanted and enchained by the pleasure of a song, soon the cicadas will start buzzing again.

6.

30 April 2011.

From the outer edge of some buried age, a small print stares at me from the corner of my desk. It stares from a rectangular shape made of Japanese watercolour paper, edges torn. Against a bright yellow and partly erased background, two teal doodles hover one on top of the other. At the bottom, one word in light brown small letters:

Listen.

That a flat print is prompting me so directly to listen might seem an awkward proposition in itself. That the two teal zigzagging shapes now take the shape in my mind of two small and squashed loudspeakers, only reinforces the short circuit between seeing and hearing, enacted by this work – at least, in my reading of it. Or shall I say in my hearing of it?

The first time I interviewed Steve Roden, the author of this print, I asked him about listening and silence. It wasn't much of a philosophical enquiry, but a specific question about a project called *vascellum*, in the 1999 anthology *Site of Sound: of Architecture & the Ear*, where Steve had chosen to reproduce two drawings of a small speaker. A speechless object made to channel sound but not generating sound in itself: to see it appear in a drawing opened up to another way of channelling sound, indirect and imagined. Steve wrote to me that *vascellum* was about the activity of listening, which lies at the foundation of many of his works.

Vascellum in Latin means vessel, both a small ship and a container; and indeed Steve's drawings both channel imagined sounds and ambient sounds, and contain them as possibilities, as gentle prompts to listening. In his long engagement with silent media, Steve is well at ease in the absence of sound – and when sound does appear in his works it seems saturated with silence, each of its particles sifted or absorbed by a myriad quiet moments of reading, of looking, of hearing.

Steve was one of the very first artists I came across in the late nineties, when I began to explore what looked like a blurred territory between art and sound. In a very intuitive manner I was trying to connect Steve's records, drawings, sound installations and paintings. I was interested not in the why, but in the way these pieces would all converge – not just in my imagination and experience, but also in my writing around them.

Over a decade of dialogue with Steve I learned a lot about his language and his method, and I thought a lot about reading and listening in relation to writing. I began a silent, resonating engagement with the space of words in its relationship with an elusive matter such as sound. I began to write from the side of somebody who listens. Sound appeared as a perceptual asymptote for my words: they would tend constantly to it, they would be forever disjointed from it.

Often a book is a starting point for Steve. As he operates on the form and the structure of a text, not drawing from any authoritative notion of meaning, he infuses his own voice – literally and metaphorically – within the pre-existing words. It happens in *fallen / spoken,* the ongoing project he started in 2000 on finding a second-hand book by the Swedish poet Pär Lagerkvist. Not knowing Swedish, he decided to attempt a series of *intuitive translations* in which each poem in the book would generate a new text in English, physically and textually dependent on the original. *And so I began poem by poem, writing in the book itself, and trying to find logic in a word and its use, perhaps several times in a single poem. The first poem –* Angest, angest ar min arvedel *– went relatively smoothly, in that* angest *could easily become* angels, min *become* small *(related to miniature), and* arvedel *sounded a lot like* marvellous... *so it became* Angels, angels small and marvellous... Sar *became* stars, strupes *became* stripes, varlden *became* verdancy, *and so on.*

My main interest was in creating a space of intimate wandering, where one has to get close not only to read and see, but to begin to approach the activity of listening with the same intimate response as reading and looking, Steve wrote about his project *when books are like butterflies.* He used every description of sounds and colours in Georges Rodenbach's book *Bruges-la-Morte* as a score to generate a sound piece, a text and a series of images. I think of this intimate space for listening as I go back to Steve's *speak no more about the leaves,* a CD inspired by Arnold Schönberg's *The Book of the Hanging Gardens* and the poems by Stefan George used by the composer as lyrics. In the first track Steve dissected one of George's poems by syllables, which he put in alphabetical order and backwards, and then vocalised. In the second track he used the vowel structure in the poem as the score to strike five small chimes. The result is an ancient-sounding texture, woven by the voice and its recurring waves. *Meaning* is made of particles of sound, it's ingrained in the materiality of voice and its melodies. *Understanding* too lies within the substance of words as they are spoken or drawn upon a page, within their sparse rhythmic arrangements.

Steve's encounters with his source materials – objects, sounds, maps, songs, books, postcards – do not act as external references: they are the forces that move each piece. His works unfold through quiet interactions with surfaces, and call for any presence enwrapped by them and hovering around them. And yet he does not impose a backwards decoding activity on his viewers and listeners: his creative process is more akin to a transformation that includes unpredictable decisions, and the rigour of the system never gets in the way of eyes and ears. Each reference is worked through layers of transformations and digressions, not as a quick appropriation of an external other but as the result of a long dedication.

Every time I get close to a new work by Steve I encounter

something vaguely familiar but blurred, and I rediscover lost memories as they reappear filtered by years and experience. It is a nuance in his way with colours, an inflection in his aural arrangements, a distinctive cadence of thought and eye, which imbue his words and sounds and paintings and seem to come from far away, from the outer edge of some buried age – just like when once, down a lost alley in an old village, I saw a stone step out of place, and a broken buttress with no weight upon itself, and wonder why they were there; and then I no longer thought of the why, but of the way they were there. I began to trace other architectures around them, and to think of other ways I could see around things.

Long-lasting impressions seep out of Steve's works, unveiled, glanced off.

They stay and resurface as quiet apparitions, as frayed icons.

5.

23 January 2011.

I think of reference in Writing Sound as I read Chapter Two in *Pandora's Hope* by Bruno Latour, entitled *Circulating Reference*: the French sociologist describes the procedures carried out by soil science experts and geographers to translate soil samples from a forest into a map of a forest, and compares such procedures to the use of reference: *to pack the world into words*, he says. In the same chapter Latour shows how *in losing the forest we win knowledge of it*. I would like to draw a parallel between the transition from forest to map and the transition from listening to writing, with particular regards to the function of reference: that is, packing into words the world of listening, while being removed from it.

In losing a sound we gain knowledge of it: in words.

+

3 May 2011.

In Latin the verb *referre* means *to bring back*, and this bringing back occurs across layers of transformations. Latour further clarifies such process of transformation in a recent article, looking at how the correspondence between territory and map does not occur as an abstraction, but *in practice* and through reference. He writes of the navigator, who works out a route not based on some abstract correspondence between map and territory, but on the detection of cues on site and in real time between one steppingstone and the next. Each detection is not a *deadly jump* but a *deambulation*: a walk through and about a number of steppingstones. The gap between two steps is packed with reference to layers of experience and observations; with laboured operations, detours or even falls and dead ends.

The metaphor of walking about, and specifically the use of

the term *deambulation,* appear fittingly with regards to my story and my approach to Writing Sound, as I move around a landscape of listening moments and transform it: a walk through and about the changing landscape of a listening experience as it is recalled in words, through reference to layers of knowledge, moments of being, of forgetting and of undoing, as they're attached to an inner landscape, and onto these pages. I organise and circulate reference as necessary to the shaping of my writing, as it is woven into the very texture of my writing until it can no longer be disjoined. Until I interweave *in its proper place a darker thread with the story as publicly narrated.* Until both my story as a writer and my story as a reader are woven into the fabric of these pages, their darker threads mixed with the main plot.

Writing Sound advocates variety and it opens up to multiplicity of outcomes. It presents and propagates one's history. It is shaped across one's personal experiences, collections and recollections of words and sounds and places.

This is why I take my words for a walk in the fluctuating landscape of the same city over and over, this is why I go on rambling through my archive of words and sounds.

To stop walking around them means they will no longer be audible.

4.

5 May 2011.

Do I need any more than this? Do I need silence now? How do I listen? These questions inhabited my mind on sorting out and packing my collection of records twice within two years. They also spawned the following reflections on going back to certain listening places, and on listening as a landscape to return to and reshape. On listening again. On listening, again.

+

A most dreaded moment. A friend calls me and asks, *So, have you listened to anything* new *this month?*

I waver in a state of confusion.

I haven't got anything to reply. I am speechless at my friend's expectations. She genuinely believes I can open up new listening dimensions on her behalf.

As if.

I try to get back in the conversation, and stammer out of my broken voice, *Er... well... I have been listening again to* The Man-Machine.

Silence on the other side.

Yes, I've been listening again to The Man-Machine, I repeat, starting to feel like a mean machine aiming at my friend's best intentions. It is the truth, but it doesn't seem to provoke anything more than bafflement, or a cold ironic remark. Maybe my friend knows all that record by heart, maybe it is not *of the moment* for her to speak of Kraftwerk, and that machine is covered with a thick layer of dust. At this point my friend hangs up, after some generic appreciation of *Ah, Kraftwerk!*'s dystopian vision. I start thinking that if I'd mentioned listening to the washing machine, coated with cosy notions of domestic soundscape morphing into alienation, my friend might have been much, much happier.

She rings again the following week and, more prepared to counter her inquisitive assault, I mention having listened again to *Bella Ciao*. Yes, the collection of traditional workers' chants and partisan songs from Italy, published after the 1964 edition of the Spoleto Festival.

Now I hear a reproach, *Nostalgic communist!*, in my friend's embarrassed silence. For the sake of friendship, at this point I resist the seducing temptation of mentioning an old collection of choirs from World War I, sung by a choir of Alpine soldiers.

So, you don't have anything more special *in mind? Or... anything more* new? As if the only point was about listening to *special, new* music.

Nothing special. What is special about this nothing is how I get there, and what I make of the experience of listening every time I return. Every time haunted or charged by the past, every time informed by the new: a progression of moments of awareness accumulated into the now, with all its load of then's.

To listen again. To recognise and to discover more, until I realise how immediate and how singular each listening experience is. Like when I travel back to a landscape known and surprising at once, thrilled at the thought of returning and concerned at the thought of finding myself a stranger in what once was familiar. To listen again consolidates a sense of *being there* as I listen. Hence Kraftwerk, *Bella Ciao*, the Alpine choir: at different points they have signified in turn losses and returns, they shaped my attention and my approach to listening. On my way to school in a cold winter, *Kling-Klang, Kling-Klang, Kling-Klang*, pacing myself and my intentions to the sounds of *Metropolis*; at home with my family in my childhood, when the partisan songs in *Bella Ciao* and the Alpine soldiers' songs from World War I meant nothing more than a shared sense of rhythm, and refrain, and belonging.

The act of listening is like a forgotten currency, which I can use to buy *the most precious, priceless nothing*: an ever-changing, ever-familiar experience. I go through or skip away from loops I believed I could sing along; I listen to what I thought I'd misheard, I overhear what I thought I'd heard, I find myself distracted in points that once took all my attention, I rejoice again at certain turns and bends.

I am surprised every time by every listening moment as by every return: familiar and new, always present and singular.

3.

2 December 2010.

I am listening to Chiara Guidi leading a workshop. I am listening to Elizabeth Cotten.

They disappear into their voices, singing.

Chiara, an actress, speaks of her technique to find a voice to interpret a given text. Elizabeth, a singer – or rather her voice, creaking out of two speakers – sings *Freight Train*.

Elizabeth is the woman from North Carolina – a self-taught left-handed guitarist – who at the beginning of the last century developed a technique to play her instrument upside down: melodies on bass strings, bass line with the fingers on the high strings. *They won't know what route I've gone.* I listen to her voice and not bother about that freight train. How does her voice inhabit words?

Chiara is the woman from Cesena, Italy, who shakes theatre audiences worldwide with myriad voices. Calling for the voice of Elizabeth in her workshop, she seems to operate in a similar manner: she plays the bass lines of a text with the tips of her voice, she plays the melodies with the bass chords in her throat. How does her voice inhabit words?

Chiara's point is not about interpreting a text. She lets her voice find her way through herself first. A voice is always shaped out of somewhere else, outside; at the same time it comes from her body and her history, from the experiences that move her. Chiara's main search has to do with inhabiting words, not with being inhabited by them. Her reading swarms with voices as she channels and modulates them. It is not about clinging to the text as a fixed object of truth dictating one single voice, but about giving way to the experiences that allow her to move freely inside it. It is not about reading as an act of submission, but about *putting her hands inside the substance of words. Meaning* comes in a lot later. When she says *I* it is in fact *they*. *They* are her collection of voices and sounds. They outline the landscape in which her voice moves.

Chiara speaks of a *molecular* search into her voice across two parallel landscapes: the one depicted in the given text, and the one she places herself into while trying to visualise her own voice every day. In the same manner, when she works with students on a classic piece of theatre, she won't go on about theories on Shakespeare, or *Macbeth*: she will just give the students the words to read. The words, not the text. The words as living entities onto which each reader can respond to, as a living entity: not the text as a fixed keeper of a still truth. The words and their particles, carrying *all those concrete details of life that make actual the mystery of our position on earth.*

Chiara's method has got no interpretation, claims for authority or stated insight attached. Every day she transcribes and imitates a sound that catches her attention; she attempts to outline its margins. Each sound is placed under the same level of inspection, like coldly observed raw materials: no hierarchical arrangement gets in the way of her feeling, knowing, and understanding. Each sound is encountered in a backward walk toward the individual inner strength of words: Chiara entitled her workshop *Report on the Backward Truth of Voice.*

By choosing Cotten's *Freight Train* to accompany her workshop Chiara seems to say: listen. Pay attention to this voice and to what moves it. Do not strive to see that freight train. If today you feel your body is in a jungle, then feel the jungle, move your body and your voice with it across the jungle, attach your movement in the jungle to the movement of the voice and then, finally, of the train. The train will end up moving because you find your drive within your personal experience. If you feel tangled, the movement of your voice will arise as you cut through the vegetation. It will never arise from studying the singer's intentions, or the way the engine of a freight train works.

I see this manner of operation as tightly attached to a will to channel and resurrect words. To resurrect still, dead words from the page you have to want to get close to the real stuff that can animate them, not just their stiff image. You have to want to deal with sounding them. You need to remind people of when they really felt for something, or somebody. Likewise to animate the dead heap of words buried within my collection of books, I need to breathe my own voice into them. Channel them out of my inner landscape.

In the late nineteenth century Gerard Manley Hopkins spoke of a force – he called it *instress* – that moves each individual (and plant, and thing) and makes each one remarkably unique. It seems to me that Chiara too urges to find, and to voice one's own *instress*: the force holding up one's words and entire being.

I tie Chiara's and Hopkins's words into an idea of landscape as being insisted upon and modified by personal instances of reading and of listening. Hopkins also coined the word *inscape*, to name the *individually-distinctive* form that reveals the uniqueness of each being. The *instress* not only makes up the individual being as such, but also denotes the impulse that moves from the *inscape* on to the senses and on to the viewer and the listener: it is the unexpected and intermittent perception of a recurring pattern, which gives sense and which moves.

My inscape is attached to these pages; my history of listening and reading moments takes on various features in the attempt of raising these written lines into a place. It is a collection of encounters with pages and places; a recollection, mixed with invention but true to its score. It conveys the sense of shaping, step by step along the journey of the reading and listening I, my words out of nothing other than the pace of a rhythm, into a land of visions both ancient and new, familiar and strange.

2.

7 May 2011.

Once more I consider the vexed question of reference in Writing Sound. Today I found a possible key to this, as I listened again to a track by Mike Cooper. It is entitled *The New Urban Hula Slide* and it enters like a distorted apparition at the end of his 2004 masterpiece of expanded exotica, *Rayon Hula*.

Birdsong comes from all over, and voices are barely audible. An inverted rhythm stumbles upon itself. A heavenly tune on lap steel guitar is set against tape loops reversing a typical Arthur Lyman Hawaiian melody. In the moments of silence a croak, a bark, a caw, a chirp dot over this sonic texture, mad and wild. Is it the song of hoopoe, chaffinch, turtle dove? There is nothing reassuring here, other than the disjointed movement of this track's own unravelling. Halfway through, the muffled sound of an engine is heavily incorporated in the piece. Birdsong again and, two minutes later, birdsong. *Upupa Epops, Fringilla Coelebs, Streptopelia Turtur*? No foreground or background: all is resolved and contained in its own complex flatness, animated by the rhythm of its recurring patterns and not by its depth. Birdsong builds up. No more melody in the last two minutes: just the strident cohabitation of sounds and flashes of variously pitched noises. At some point it stops. It doesn't fade out: it stops. Back to point zero, I listen again. What could be read as background noise versus melody, exist together in the mesmerising flatness of their unity, and of their patterned repetition. Ambient sounds, melody and tape loops move on the same plateaux: they are not subordinated to one another, they are one. What occurs around the music is as relevant as the music itself.

Mike once told me *Rayon Hula* is about listening to what goes on around you together with the music, about delving into listening to the world around as much as listening to what you assume you should be listening to. The main issue for him is not

I am making music, but *I am weaving a texture,* within a daily practice saturated with sound vision taste feel travel return. He calls for the listener before the musician and music for him is not a grand statement: it channels a diffused mood, not made just of sounds but of visions, incidental noises, colours, stories, traditions, lyrics, images in motion.

The experience of listening is inclusive and so is my writing of it. When writing of a musician like Mike, I need to bring in all the reference in his world, *what happens around,* until it is ingrained in the very substance of my words in the same manner as the ambient sounds are ingrained in the very substance of Mike's music. I do not seek to convey an experience of sound as such, pure and devoid, but rather a precipitation into the multi-coloured and distorted vortex of Mike's influences. I need to retain those colours and those patterns, those images and those ambient noises.

Mike's recordings, pursued across his long and frequent journeys to the South-East of Asia and Oceania, drizzle with the most solar, languid aspects of his travels alongside the darker ones, in tarry hells made of disturbed loops, hard-to-pin-down field recordings and deconstructed sonic constellations. His complex language never falls into decorative temptation, but is rooted in a density of experiences as they accumulate in time, and in the trespassing of stylistic borders. His work is not just philological: it gives form to imagined landscapes, in the interplay and the ambiguity of natural and artificial sounds. The result is never pure, it's very contaminated, and so is the approach to music making: all the colours shapes movements precipitate into the texture and the grain of the sound, just like the patterns in the Hawaiian shirts that Mike has been collecting for over thirty years.

Rayon Hula is not only dedicated to Lyman but also to Ellery Chun, the inventor of the *aloha shirt.* The patterns in each shirt are repeated and each shirt is a loop in itself, a repetition of an image on a piece of fabric. Mike explained me how the art of the *aloha shirt* design is in fact a fake. *The Hawaiians, like the Balinese, adapt their culture to suit people. Hawaiian shirts were initially manufactured out of kimono fabrics made in Hawaii. In the 1930's Chun realised that tourists liked to wear those patterns, so they became* Hawaiian, *and the* aloha shirt *was born.*

The *traditional* Hawaiian shirt appears to be a fake. Is there any claim for authenticity in this picture? What is real and what is fake in Mike's repeating patterns? I'd rather shift the question to the texture assembled in such a hybrid operation between fake and tradition. The complexity of these patterns is inherent in the weaving of its own fabulation. Rather than interrogating its provenance, I'd let myself be enthralled in this vortex of images and sounds as they reshape and actually make *a* tradition, every time anew.

1.

9 May 2011.

Golden leaves gleam, dishevelled against a cloudy sky. There is still something raw and aching about these clouds although they are vanishing. The entire scene seems covered by a soaked damp veil. Above and below and in the distance and in the forefront, everything is still wet with rain, but again it starts shimmering.

I first wrote these words to attempt and report my layers of recollections of the Protestant Cemetery in Rome and its landscape. As I write of my repeated listening moments in the Cemetery through the filter of Pasolini's verses and of my memories, what I outline cannot be but a stratified construction of all the thoughts and words and sounds, that have been with me on every visit through the years and that hit my every return – my every now, with its load of then's amassed on it.

There is no claim for authenticity or immediacy in my picture of the Cemetery. It doesn't matter what is real and what is fake in its repeating patterns. I shift the glance and the ear to its texture, woven in such a hybrid operation. Rather than interrogating the provenance and aim of this scene, I'd let myself be enthralled in this vortex of recalled and revisited images, sounds and words. I no longer know what was real and what I imagined, what I heard and what I made myself believe I was hearing. I construct a place, I channel a presence as a frayed palimpsest of notated experiences, anticipations, recollections.

+

10 May 2011.
I read again an interview I did with Keith Rowe six years ago.

He talked to me of his concern with the notion of profundity in today's music: a question that sounds crucial in his attempt to perforate the flatness of the digital realm. *How to convey profundity through a surface?*, he wondered. And, I would add, dynamics through stillness, repetition through deambulation?

By laying the guitar on the table, Keith told me in reply to a question about *Duos for Doris*, the 2003 album he recorded with John Tilbury, *I have access to long sounds. Immediately I think of the basso continuo in the Baroque music tradition: I could think of myself as a* basso continuo *player and of John as a harpsichord player, his notes above the* basso continuo. *Then I begin to think of other elements in Baroque music: its sonority, its very sour, bitter quality, and* canto fermo, *plainchant, a melody that goes under the basso continuo but so slowly that only God can hear it. Where is this profundity, this* canto fermo, *in what we do? Is there, or can there be a profound meaning in electronic music? There is no answer. But it is crucial to ask.*

+

11 May 2011.

Listening and writing are bound to remain strangers to each other, and Writing Sound inhabits the space of this otherness. There is no prescriptive way of being in such a space because it is ultimately the space of memory, personal and constructed in the present.

I think of writing sound as the space of an absence, strictly tied to the act of remembering: and how does memory take shape? To remember means to construct an impression of a lost presence; moreover, often memory has to do with the desire of a memory, thus questioning any claim for an origin that prescribes a one-sided faithfulness to it. Think for example of that part in Proust's *Recherche* when the narrator recalls his first meeting with Gilberte, and says, *If her eyes hadn't been so dark, I would have not loved in her, as I did, especially her blue eyes.* Here the presumed authenticity of Gilberte's black eyes fades in the authenticity of the narrator's vision of blue eyes, and both merge in a memory that is written and constructed through the experience of a place: the hiss of the wind, the hues and smells of the pink hawthorns, all contributing to the construction of the recollection.

Each memory, hence each memory of a sound, is mediated, filtered, deferred – and yet, present every time it is written. Sounds cannot be separated from a sense of place, and writing sound in turn is not concerned with abstractions only manifested to the ears, detached and purely aural: writing embraces sound as it calls for the participation of deepest perceptions, desires and further recollections, and possesses us to the point when we no longer know what we heard and what we think we'd heard. Ultimately, what we know is what we write.

Sounds as sounds will stay as such. To write sound has to do with our *not being in sounds;* our memories of them speak of the places where we experience them in time. What we exchange as humans are our reports mixed with our longing, our words and the words of others: stories of stories, constructions of constructions.

The landscape of writing sound appears like a *mise en abîme* with blurred margins, where the frame of each new scene fades into the next and is not clearly defined: where memories and words from the past are renewed into the now. As I write sound, what I outline cannot be but a layered construction of all the thoughts and words and images that have been with me through the years within the landscapes of my listening, and that load my every return. There is no claim for authenticity, it doesn't matter what is real and what is fake in the texture woven in such a hybrid operation. Rather than interrogating the provenance and aim of the resulting text I'd lose myself in its patterns of recalled, reinvented and revisited scenarios, in words. What matters is what is here / what I hear today, when I construct my writing sound as a *mise en abîme* of eroding and revived experiences, anticipations, recollections.

I go back to Calvino's lonely king. Despite of the illusion of dialogic space encountered in his duet, at the end he wakes up in a cave underground. Once more alone, once more with his buzz in his head, once more uncertain of his status and place. The circularity of reaching out, through words, and yet being entrenched in the uniqueness of each listening moment, is the space of writing sound. It is prompted by a question, *Where am I?* It enquires about a place, and it constructs over and over the landscape in which I locate myself, or lose myself – personally, culturally – every time I set out to write after listening. It opens incremental horizons through the singularities of each telling. It doesn't have to do with prescriptive ways, all-encompassing categories or defining reasons, but with the presence of an experience and of a place, in the intermittences, the raptures and the falls of every other today.

+

12 May 2011.

As a listener I uncover new layers of profundity in sound and I weave them all together in the surface of my inscape: all the strata of words, sounds, memories exist in the same place as I write them. After I've deambulated, descended, reached the edges, I pack layers of reference on the surface of my words, I draw the lines of my inscape.

Now I think back of the day I received that postcard from Ethel, and things become much clearer as I scan again its surface and precipitate in its depths. I search for a *canto fermo*, for a bass hum in the underground passages and caves, and I record it as it seeps through the surface of my inscape.

CHAPTER 7

TO THE EDGE AND FALLING

FROM THE NOTEBOOKS ON WRITING

SOUND

10.

13 May 2011.

From the outer edge of a buried age, continue to write.

9.

14 May 2011.

The Domus Aurea in Rome does not lie too far from the beginning of via Appia. Art historians would mention the effect of the discovery of its wall paintings on the late school of Raphael and on that twisted side of early Mannerism developed in the sixteenth century around the workshops of Giovanni da Udine and Baldassarre Peruzzi. Underground, I follow another clue. As I revisit the grotesques in those wall paintings I see holes on the ceilings and the vaults, and I'm reminded of how the Domus Aurea was rediscovered at the end of the fifteenth century after a long period of oblivion: by a boy falling accidentally into a hole, as he walked on the hill above the site. The falling is as important as the discovery: an image of a process related as much to a sense of motion, as to the accident of *being there* and finding.

I've been walking to the edge and I've been falling. Once I've precipitated, I look up at the ceiling of my making – of my seeing, reading, listening, writing. There, I can see some old pictures, beautifully crafted or a bit battered; other times it is detritus, scratched walls, crumbling plasters, incomplete images, emerging patches of grey and cerulean mould. These pages are like those Roman walls and like those ceilings underground. Ethel's postcard was one of those holes. I fell into a hall of resounding spaces and now I deambulate, stuck in the locked grooves of some recurring memories, getting over my *damnatio memoriae* of a city.

8.

15 May 2011.

At Bologna University in the early forties Pasolini attended the classes led by Roberto Longhi, the noted art historian who spoke of a Realist line of tradition in Italian painting linking fourteenth-century schools of Northern Italy to Caravaggio. A strong advocate of a formalist approach to art, Longhi wrote of paintings representing life as *a daily drama of forms and gestures set up in an irrefutable space, under a joyful, nearly accusing light*; he wrote of paintings that depict a humanity unconstrained and abrupt, as the faces of real people lend their features to those of saints and martyrs. Longhi offered Pasolini a way of seeing and of comprehending, by means of visual art, realistic aspects of figurative tradition in Italy; in turn, Pasolini called the effect of his meeting with the art historian a *figurative fulguration*, acknowledged by him in the opening credits of *Mamma Roma*.

The exaggerated realism of the tableaux vivants in *La ricotta* is a product of both Longhi's teachings, and of Pasolini's reading of a line of poetic tradition stemming from the thirteenth-century languages of Jacopone da Todi and Tommaso da Celano, whose *Dies Irae* he would use in the film. In one of his early poems, written in the Friulano dialect from the area in North-Eastern Italy where he spent his childhood, Pasolini had evoked an image of Christ: *Vegnerà el vero Cristo, operaio / A insegnarte a ver veri sogni. The real Christ, a worker, will come / To teach you to see real dreams.*

The assonance between *ver* and *veri* – *to see* and *real* – reinforces the verse's focus on the oxymoron, *real dreams*. Pasolini's *real Christ* is the connection between seeing reality and visions; like in *La ricotta* many years later, it places viewers in the middle of the explosions of tangibility (see), the bright colours of a *figurative fulguration* (real) and implausible apparitions (dreams).

7.

16 May 2011.

At once, sublime and of earth earthy. I borrow these words from Joris-Karl Huysmans' description, in *Là-bas, Down There,* of the *Tauberbischofsheim Altarpiece* by Matthias Grünewald. I'm not referencing the actual painting or the actual book, but the state of closeness enacted by Huysmans in the scene of his writing the painting inside the book. I'm interested most of all in putting my writing self in the same place as Huysmans; to assimilate his way of looking, although I'm looking at – in fact, recalling – a different picture, Pontormo's *Deposition.*

Writing sound takes on more and more the aspect of a question: *Where am I?.* It enquires about the space in which I choose to locate myself, or to lose myself, when I set out to write in response to a sound, a book, a picture, a place. It doesn't have to do with a reason, a before, a why, but with a presence, an experience, a way, now.

6.

17 May 2011.

World War I: a palimpsest of songs and words and visions. I let the voice of my personal Siren, *The Captain's Testament*, breathe into Ungaretti's war poem *Vigil* and against the backdrop of Baziotes' grinning, mutilated *Dwarf* until I no longer know where the voice of one ends and the other's begins, until they all merge into a new accretion in unsteady unison, vaguely familiar to one another and yet strongly stranger to one another. They become animated by connections between seeing and reading, poetry and painting – unexpected and electric. It is not synaesthesia but cohabitation of worlds, which exist because I weave another story around them. Sometimes the cohabitation might be a bit out of phase, other times one voice matches quite seamlessly the shape of the other voice, of the other writing or painting – it is, after all, a new imaginary construction, whose presence is disclosed in my reading of it. Framed by blurred margins, it is a hypnotising repetition, a distorted echo chamber where each new scenario fades out into the next.

The captain of the company is wounded and just about to die, and sends the news to his Alpine soldiers, so that they come and find him. *A WHOLE night thrown near the body of a slain comrade, his mouth snarling ... his clawed fingers ripping into my silence.* I command that my body is CUT IN FIVE PIECES. The first piece to my Country, the second piece to the battalion, the third piece to my mother, so that she remembers her son. The fourth piece to my beautiful one, so that she remembers her first love, the last piece to the mountains, so that they cover it with roses and flowers.

5.

26 February 1998.

Intermittently recalling Ungaretti again. *...body of slain comrade, mouth snarling ... clawed fingers ripping into my silence...*

4.

5 March 1998.

As I think and hear through the surface of Baziotes' *Dwarf*, I realise how certain paintings appear to be made of a substance so finely attuned to one of my thoughts, that they infiltrate the mind till I no longer know what I see and what I imagine I'm being seduced into seeing, what I hear and what I imagine I'm being seduced into hearing. Here are the recollections of my mind, responding to a silent painting in which I make myself believe a fantastic creature appears to be listening to something – a voice, a melody, a memory? I indulge in the thought that the voice of my personal Siren surfaces out of this canvas, slowly progressing toward the front.

It is the mysterious that I love in my painting. It is the stillness and the silence. I want the picture to take effect very slowly, to obsess and to haunt, Baziotes wrote. All his life he went about to outline a primordial world of solitary figures across layers of symbolic and personal meaning. In a letter to Alfred H. Barr discussing a series of pictures including *Dwarf* he wrote, *I think these forms are inspired from having looked at the lizards and prehistoric animals*. The expression is *a mixture of horror and humour … He has a certain coldness, a certain deadliness, the eyes of a madman aren't too far from a lizard's, unknown, unscrupulous, inhuman*.

There was talk in New York in the forties, of cycloptic eyes switching on the internal landscape, and of psychic morphology. It was channelled by artists such as Roberto Matta and Gordon Onslow-Ford, the former with his notion of *inscape* related to his paintings, and of psychic morphology as a sequence of explosive convulsions configured within a scenery that pulsates and rotates rhythmically; the latter in his four lectures held at the New School for Social Research in 1941, in which he encouraged artists to *switch on the cycloptic eye to look inside yourselves at the internal landscape*.

3.

25 February 1998.

Today I received a postcard from Ethel:

Monday, February 9th, 1998
Very dear D.,
I have supreme confidence in you.
Baziotes and I loved the Roman wall paintings in the
Metropolitan – we returned to them again and again.
Stay close to Leonardo, Giorgione and St. Francis who loved
the harp.
I hold your hand.
Love, Ethel B.
Persevere – Stay close to the abyss.

I hear an apparition and its colour is white. It comes to me as I
think of the Roman wall paintings mentioned in Ethel's postcard.
It does not really matter where those walls belong. The place
might be New York, Rome or Pompeii; it might be a projection
from the museology shelf in my library, an attempt at outlining
the space of Ethel's memories, a spatial story of a visit to the Met
or the anticipation of a visit that might not have happened yet. In
fact it doesn't even matter, if I never visited those rooms. Those
blacks, whites and reds, that cycloptic eye, flatness and vertigo
might resurface later on, if I allow to push myself to imagined
spaces by means of reading, and to imagined sounds by means of
records – records or, in other words, words.

2.

19 May 2011.

Addosso is an Italian adverb, translated in English as *over*. What goes missing in the translation is the sense of movement inherent in the Italian word that implies etymologically (*dosso* means *shoulders*) a motion forward, embracing at once. As I revisit my notes about listening and reading and writing, I replace the notion of *writing about* with one of *writing over, addosso*. I write over words, paintings, sounds, places. I need to convey the sense of closeness to what I write about, most of all the way reading, listening and recalling converge inevitably into writing. As I read and listen, my words are reflected onto my inscape across my collection of books and sounds. I can't escape any of them; my thoughts are entrenched in this syncretistic array of words from the past.

I try to write over Ethel's voice until I no longer know where my voice ends and hers begins, until the two voices merge into a new accretion in unsteady unison, vaguely familiar to each other and yet strongly stranger to each other. Sometimes this proximity might be a bit out of phase, other times one voice matches quite seamlessly the shape of the other voice, of the other writing – it is a new imaginary construction, whose presence is disclosed in my reading of it.

My words fade into those of Pasolini, Melville, Gadda. I do not call for them as frameworks of legitimacy: I rest another layer upon them and I bring them back inside my inscape, I let them point at my rhythm. I make them audible again as I intermittently inhabit them, in reading and in writing, like Melville's *Pierre*. The edges of still hidden writing undo the novel and show up its awkward functioning. In the space of reading, still hidden voices coexist and prompt to write.

...how swiftly and how wonderfully, he reads all the

obscurest and most obliterate inscriptions he finds in his memory; yea, and rummages himself all over, for still hidden writings to read.

1.

20 May 2011.

In the reading of a painting, in the reading of a piece, my point of view is an entrance that lets in the works I approach, as they contribute to the unfolding of my story. The words of Pasolini or Gramsci enter my inscape as I write them in it, across my memories and at a certain time. I reshape them every time I breathe my reading voice into them.

Today I read again my university dissertation, which brought about my meeting with Ethel. The focus of it was a magazine edited by artists, writers and musicians in New York in the forties. *Possibilities*, it was called. I begin to understand how that research was prompted by weaving a connective tissue around all those different languages, in words, around and over recurring references. In reading and listening today I generate relationships among words and sounds in my archive, and consolidate such relationships through writing. A cobweb, a frayed pattern of images, words, sounds envelop each new page together with the experience that originates it. The movement is one of inclusion; it keeps very close to the materials I use, to how they are, how they feel, how they sound.

+

21 May 2011.

Recorded and recalled in the pages of these notebooks and back into a succession of listening moments, in my memory Ethel's voice does not appear as a permanent entity: it hovers in a hesitant space of change, as a presence delineated by a fluctuating movement of estrangement and recognition: when Ethel said *I* it was in fact *they*. *They* were her memories of voices, of words, of sounds. They outlined the landscape in which her voice moved.

I try to write Ethel's voice as if I was recording a number of aural ruminations in spite of myself, encountering myself as a foreigner. The moment of recognition comes some time later, when I realise how the mutable matter of my listening moments has to be kept together by the very sense of dissipation that permeated the words to which Ethel gave shape.

My inscape is attached to these pages; it is a collection of encounters with words and places; a recollection, mixed with invention but true to its score. It conveys the sense of shaping, step by step along the journey of the reading I, the blank page out of nothing other than the pace of a rhythm, into a land of visions both ancient and new, familiar and strange.

+

22 May 2011.

Each page of this book now appears like a newly discovered edge of my inscape. The same clusters of words take on different aspects and visit different places; they are moved by the same core drive to deambulate up to those edges.

This is not the outpouring of an autobiographical image: it is an image distorted, reiterated, projected, reinvented and echoed into clusters of words. And not even just one image but clouds of them, attached to the same landscape. It has to do with remembering and returning, today and every other today; with the fixed rhythmic gestures that move my listening, my reading and my writing, where the formulaic quality of certain recurring images outline the limits within which I can say *I* again. This is a *katabasis*: in Greek, both the movement of going underground, and the movement from the inner land to the coast – the movement of my words to the edges of an inscape.

Part 111

CHAPTER 8

LAMENT

1.

I want to tell you of a song.

It is entitled *Lament for the Death of Pasolini* and it follows the structure of a traditional extra-liturgical religious ballad from Central Italy, the *Prayer of Saint Donatus*. It was written in December 1975 after Pier Paolo Pasolini's death by an Italian singer called Giovanna Marini. It begins like this: *I lost all of my strength, I lost my ability.*

At some point about three years ago I lost all my strength and my ability. I no longer could see a consistent picture in all I'd done and written over the previous ten years. What had appeared until then like a congruous body of work, crumbled in a myriad scattered pieces that I knew I had to stitch together again.

As I read, as I listen and as I write, I am engulfed in an assonant riddle. It hovers between *chi sono?* – in Italian meaning both *who am I?* and *who are they?* – and *chi suono?* – *whom do I sound?* – voicing the aural universe where my research moves. Many questions, infested by many *who's*. These pages swarm with the voices of those questions, and when I say *I* it is in fact *they*: my archive of voices, of words, of sounds, outlining the landscape in which I move. I inhabit my landscape of readings and of listening moments, at times as a guest, at times as a stranger, at times as a parasite, at times as a ghost. I go for a walk around my favourite places of listening, I look for another way of understanding, and of stitching those broken pieces together. Until I reach the edge of an abyss.

Ethel's words: *Persevere, stay close to the abyss.*

2.

As I listen again to Marini's *Lament* I think of the Lament as a form of collective mourning, studied and outlined by the Italian ethnographer Ernesto de Martino in his 1958 book *Morte e pianto rituale nel mondo antico, Death and Ritual Lament in the Ancient World*. Following a number of surveys and field trips carried out in the fifties in the Lucania region of Southern Italy, de Martino traced a line of tradition in Lament whose form had persisted since the ancient rituals of mourning, and had resisted the liturgical dictates of Catholicism via a series of hybridisations of a defined canon.

The Lament is the technique of crying after somebody's death: a ritual developed by early Mediterranean civilisations to circumscribe loss within a safe, mythical horizon. It is the third stage of what de Martino identifies as a sequence of mourning. The first stage expresses a moment of wordlessness and being dumbstruck by loss; it is followed by uncontrolled crying and frenzy, and it is finally restrained in the Lament, which controls loss within a protected psychic space. Such protection is possible because of a defined structure, and because of the insistence of its refrains and formulaic expressions.

The Lament, moreover, exudes a staged quality with no claims for authenticity or for the outpouring of uncontrolled emotion: often in a funeral, groups of women *who know how to weep* enact the Lament on behalf of the family of the dead. Witnesses report how each Lament sounds as if it was not an individual woman *really* crying but another one, or any other one, *anonymous and dreamy*, who gives voice to the refrains expressing that someone died. For de Martino the woman who vocalises the Lament embodies *the ritual presence of a very particular regime of psychic duality*, where she does not pour out an autobiographical image: she is this image distorted, reiterated, projected, reinvented and echoed into clusters of words and recurring patterns. The shaping of the weeping woman's voice has to do with remembering and returning; with the fixed rhythmic gestures that move her voice, where the regularity of rhymes and the formulaic quality of certain images protect her from paroxysm and outline the limits within which human presence can be reaffirmed, in spite of incommensurable death. It is an example of the formal power of being against what moves on in nature, unmeasured.

The stronger the fixed, repeated form, the stronger the individual stories woven into this form appear, as they exceed it and perpetuate it.

+

While Pasolini was editing the collection of poems *Canzoniere Italiano, Italian Songbook,* he chose to include four chants from Lucania – the same region where he would later on film *Il Vangelo secondo Matteo, The Gospel According to St. Matthew* – belonging to de Martino's studies published prior to the *Death and Ritual Lament* book. The emphasis de Martino put on the weight of utterance, of speech, of oral culture in the shaping of the Lament, and his insistence on the fact that such form is not to be seen as a crucible of silent literary texts but as an act ingrained in a rituality of gestures, of facial expressions, of sounds and rhythms, prompted a number of reflections in Pasolini's work. During one of the tableaux vivants in *La ricotta,* for example, the Lament of Mary appears from out of the scene, in the disembodied voice of the prompter: he reads *Donna de' Paradiso, Woman of Paradise,* a thirteenth-century sacred ballad also known as *Il pianto della Madonna, The Madonna's Lament,* written by the Franciscan monk Jacopone da Todi whose style is noted for its hyperrealist descriptions in the vulgar tongue of Central Italy.

De Martino's stance is present too in the second poem of *The Ashes of Gramsci* entitled *Il canto popolare, The Popular Chant.* Here Pasolini writes of people who *take part in history only by means of an oral, magical experience*: the coexistence in a verse of the oral and the magical dimension as means to take part in history, reveals a closeness to de Martino's studies and in particular *Il mondo magico, The Magic World* published in 1948, which is the foundation for the subsequent project in Lucania. In this book de Martino discusses magic and ritual not as a manifestation out of time, but as techniques developed by people to affirm their presence in the world, and situated within the actuality of a historically loaded *now*.

3.

In *Death and Ritual Lament* de Martino also discusses the origins of the figure of the *Mater Dolorosa, the Grieving Mary,* in the representation of the Passion of Christ. The New Testament does not feature the crying of Mary as a disruptive shriek. She appears instead as a dumb spectator, stuck in poised lyricism: no uncontrolled expression of grief is reported on her face or behaviour, as early Christianity would deem any manifestations of grief for death – most of all the death of Christ – unacceptable. Only later, in apocryphal texts, the image of Mary begins to absorb pre-Christian modes of reintegration of loss, according to the ancient three-stage sequence of wordlessness, uncontrolled plaint, and Lament.

Giovanna Marini chose a non-liturgical chant to voice the loss of Pasolini. I chose her *Lament for the Death of Pasolini* as a template for this book. She chose the form of the Lament, developed independently of approved Catholic tradition – although often the two merged into hybrids between Catholic and pagan canons, and cohabited the same world. She chose a form that was still alive, in Central and Southern Italy, at the margins of the official culture, and spoke of a different world and a different attitude to death and ritual; a form that used words and expressions typical of the common speech of people – just like the faces in *La ricotta,* just like the verses and the rhythm in *Woman of Paradise.* The author of those verses, Jacopone da Todi, was also allegedly the author of the *Stabat Mater* and as I think back of this poem's opening verses – *Stabat Mater Dolorosa, iuxta Crucem lacrimosa, At the Cross her station keeping, stood the mournful mother weeping* – the outline of Marini's song takes on a stronger shape and she appears more and more as a *lacrimosa* of the people.

In her *Lament* Marini voices the impossibility of talking due to the loss of her strength and of her skill: a clear reference to the first stage of loss outlined in de Martino's *Death and Ritual Lament*. At some point she sings a verse, *O Cristo me l'hai fatto un bel disgusto, Oh Christ you have given me such a disappointment,* which nods to a line reported in the book, *Oh, ce tradimente ha fette Gesù Cristo!, Oh, what a betrayal has Jesus Christ done!* Her lament repeats patterns and refrains and stereotypes of crying: it is, by its very nature, artificial. The singer regains her strength as she voices her feelings across the fixed refrains of a traditional ballad. She inhabits an outside rhythm, she breathes her voice back into life.

I too inhabit her song: I write over it. I make a rhythm, I build a phasing, I recall a litany out of my absence, out of my return; Marini's *Lament* outlines the limits within which I can say *I* again, until my personal story exceeds its fixed refrains.

Now listen. Now look at the edges of my story and at the edges of my inscape, as I draw them from the verses of Marini's song. And then down, underground again.

4.

I lost all my strength I lost my ability. Three years ago I lost all my strength and my ability. I no longer could see a consistent picture in all I'd done and written over the previous ten years.

Death has come to visit me. Pasolini said, *Death is not about not being able to communicate / It's about no longer being understood.* What does it mean not to be understood? What does it mean to lose one's voice, to lose one's ability, to feel a stranger in one's own country?

'And lift your legs away from this kingdom'. It whispers death along this evening, it breathes in, it breathes out, in, and out, following me chasing me out of this still city of tombs. I keep listening. This still dead city of tombs is chasing me out.

Quarter past eleven I feel wounded. The captain of a company of soldiers is mortally wounded.

In front of my eyes my hands are broken. Baziotes' *Dwarf* is just one lump of matter, no limbs visible, or maybe they were mutilated.

Half past eleven I feel I'm dying. And when the sun falls down the pine trees you can still walk on these stones and there is a humming coming from below the catacombs and these slabs of history. It whispers death along this evening, it breathes in, it breathes out, in, and out, following me chasing me out of this still city of tombs. I keep listening. This still dead city of tombs is chasing me, I walk. Up to this very moment walking, listening, recalling.

My tongue would seek for words. She lets her voice find her way through herself first. That voice is always shaped out of somewhere else, outside. At the same time it comes from her own body, her history, her experience. She breathes them out as she seeks for her words.

And everything would tell me it is no good. At some point about three years ago I no longer could see a consistent picture in all I'd done and written over the previous ten years; what had appeared, until then, like a consistent body of work, crumbled in a myriad scattered pieces.

But that night I wanted to speak. I want to tell you of a song.

Alone to die there by the sea. Daniel Orme was discovered alone and dead on a height overlooking the seaward sweep of the great haven to whose shore, in his retirement from sea, he had moored.

But that night I wanted to speak. I want to tell you of a song.

5.

I researched the hagiography of Saint Donatus, whose *Prayer* Giovanna Marini shaped her *Lament* upon. Fourth century AD, Arezzo, Italy. While Donatus was celebrating mass, at the moment of communion a group of pagans entered the church and shattered the chalice. After praying, Donatus collected the fragments and put them back together; although one piece was missing from the chalice, nothing spilled out of it.

At some point about three years ago I no longer could see a consistent picture in all I'd done and written over the previous ten years; what had appeared, until then, like a whole body of work, crumbled in a myriad scattered pieces that I knew I had to stitch together again.

I've joined those fragments together again, and although the new shape might not be perfectly even, nothing will spill out of it as I write. I look for still hidden writings to read, I go back underground.

CHAPTER 9

END

*

Today I looked again at my old copy of *Pierre* and its five blank pages. I could never make a decision among those options, I couldn't find the right words to fill those pages. I then realised that each chapter in my book is made of either five or ten sections. And I recalled the result of my writing *The Captain's Testament* lyrics over Ungaretti's war poem of mutilation: A WHOLE CUT IN FIVE PIECES.

Five pieces, five pages, five sections and five sections doubled up. I will copy the sections of my book repeatedly on the five blank pages in my old Italian copy of *Pierre*. I will write over each page, until they will all appear as a trace of the experience that made them. I will once more push my words to their edge, and bring all my references back inside.

*

Golden leaves gleam, dishevelled against a cloudy sky. Deathly peace. *Among the ruins, finished the profound and naive struggle to make life over.*

I understand. Writing these pages was my walk to an edge and into a shape. Today I brought to the Protestant Cemetery my copy of *Pierre* with my words stacked inside it, I burned it and I left the ashes underneath a cypress. It was never meant to be only a book – it is today's relic of a return, it is the outline of many new projects to be, it is a remnant of my story, it is the trace of the experience that made it, and then it is a book.

I added another presence to the Cemetery and its epitaph reads, *Persevere. Stay close to the abyss.* Ethel's last sentence takes my words to the edge of my inscape.

Today looks like the end and I could start again, as I slide down the spiralling coil of this requiem. I might start from *Recordare.* To record, to recall.

*

Rome. Through rain I reached you and from rain I'm free. I can hear words and sounds from the past; the way they string the nerves like nothing else, the way they sting. They resurface with a will and a strength that exceed me. Words lost, those who reappear, those who stay like an unresolved knot of grief, those who appear in spite of a different landscape. Some things I believed I did not know are now fully grasped. They'd stayed inside like a secret, all this time. Beyond the muted freeze, beyond the grief on which these days slide, somebody else appears and I can give them these words, and listen to their other loneliness, mirror them perhaps. Minutes follow one another; time goes by. Gradually the aspect of a new event starts to appear in the shadow of another winter storm. The halo of a slowly accumulated darkness whirls over my thoughts. As my meandering thickens, so does the oncoming rain. A pool of stillness fills the air. Then finally, the wind sweeps everything away like a rush, and the low hiss of a warmer gust arises across the porticos and the stone walls, along the brick arches and the pine trees.

Maddened by red and soaked in damp twilight, in Rome today I shiver.

I think of knots of thoughts and memories and sounds, and as I revisit my memories and my places in a rosary of underground halls and far away resurgences I know: this is the only way I can see Rome today, having it hover across these marginal, resonant underground cavities and spaces that shimmer, up to the moment when my documented paths around this city merge into an apparition, down until I fall and fall and fall into the hidden catacombs and underground architectonic marvels, and what was imagined is no longer vanishing, the stone and the marble hard inside my heart and in this country, the closed-down rooms and impenetrable spaces, in the grandeur of a wonderfully orchestrated corruption, slowly, slowly, until its very truth is held at stake, until I no longer know what I'm seeing and what I am making myself believe I can see, what I'm hearing and what I am making myself believe I can hear.

References

Quotes in the book appear either embedded in the text, in italics, or as block quotations in roman type. All quotes are given credit in the following pages.

Part 1

CHAPTER 1

2.
Dickinson, Emily, 'Storm', in *Collected Poems of Emily Dickinson* (New York: Gramercy Books, 1982), 133.

4.
In 1997 I spent six months in New York to research my University dissertation for my degree in History of Art. I explored the artistic milieu in New York in the forties with focus on an art magazine, *Possibilities*, edited by William Baziotes, John Cage, Robert Motherwell. I researched the library and archive at the Museum of Modern Art and the Solomon R. Guggenheim Museum, the New York Public Library and the Artists' Papers and Oral History Program at the Archives of American Art, the Smithsonian Institution, New York branch. My references to Baziotes in this book are related to my dissertation and to my research.

Cascella, Daniela, *Possibilities I: William Baziotes, Robert Motherwell, Harold Rosenberg nella New York degli anni Quaranta*, unpublished, 1998.

Baudelaire, Charles, 'Le *Confiteor* de l'artiste', in *Petits poëmes en prose* (Milan: Rizzoli, 1990), 74. First published between 1857 and 1867.

Rosenberg, Harold, 'The shapes in a Baziotes canvas', *Possibilities* 1, 1 (1949), 2.

5.

Ungaretti, Giuseppe, 'Veglia (Cima Quattro, 23 dicembre 1915)', in *Vita d'un uomo* (Milan: Meridiani Mondadori, 1996), 25.

6.

Il Coro della S.A.T., 'Il testamento del capitano', in *Il coro della S.A.T. canta* (Milan: Odeon Carisch, 1958) [LP].

8.

La ricotta, Pier Paolo Pasolini, dir. (1963), in *Ro.Go.Pa.G.*, Roberto Rossellini, dir. (1963).

Huysmans, Joris-Karl, *Là-bas*, tr. Keene Wallace (New York: Dover Publications 1972), 12-15. First published in 1891.

9.

Roma, Federico Fellini, dir. (1972).

10.

Thoreau, Henri David, *Walden*, (Oxford: Oxford Paperbacks, 2008). First published in 1854.

The poem read by Orson Welles in *La ricotta* is part of a longer composition:

Pasolini, Pier Paolo, 'Poesie mondane', in *Poesia in forma di rosa* (Milan: Garzanti, 2001), 24. First published in 1964.

CHAPTER 2

1.

Watson, Chris, 'Stepping into the Dark. The New and Forgotten Road', CD liner notes, in *Stepping into the Dark* (London: Touch, 1996) [CD].

2.

Marini, Giovanna, 'Lamento per la morte di Pasolini (1975)', in

Correvano coi carri (Milan: I Dischi del Sole, 1979) [LP].

4.

Marini, Giovanna, 'Il mio primo incontro con Pier Paolo Pasolini', in *Cantata per Pier Paolo Pasolini* (Udine: Nota, 2000) [CD].

Marini (1979).

Il Nuovo Canzoniere Italiano, *Bella Ciao* (Milan: I Dischi del Sole, 1964) [LP].

Il Coro della S.A.T. (1958).

Marini, Giovanna, 'O Gorizia, tu sei maledetta', *Canzoni contro la guerra* [website], http://www.antiwarsongs.org/canzone.php?lang=it&id=47 accessed 12 May 2011.

Straniero, Giovanni and Barletta, Mauro, *La rivolta in musica* (Turin: Lindau, 2003).

6.

Gramsci, Antonio, *Quaderni del carcere* (XVIII), ed. Felice Platone (Turin: Einaudi 1948-1951).

Pasolini, 'Le lacrime della scavatrice', in *Le ceneri di Gramsci* (Milan: Garzanti, 2007), 73. First published in 1957.

7.

Pasolini (2007), 50.

Pasolini (2001), 24.

8.

CCCP, *Fedeli alla linea – Curami (Live a D.O.C. 1988)* [online video], 27 August 2009, http://www.youtube.com/watch?v=g RG5I4K5YRw accessed 12 May 2011.

Cage, John, *Empty Words* (Chicago: Ampersand, 2004) [2CD's].

9.

Ø, *Metri* (Helsinki: Sähkö 1994) [CD].

Conan Doyle, Arthur, 'The New Catacomb', in *Tales of Terror and Mystery* (London: John Murray, 1930), 67.

Words and expressions such as *Spargens sonum, Recordare* and *Lacrimosa*, appearing recurrently on these pages, are taken from the traditional *Sequentia* in the Requiem Mass: the *Dies Irae*, a thirteenth-century poem attributed to Tommaso Da Celano and written in Medieval Latin – one of the most exquisite examples of the leap from classic Latin metre, here based on accents and not on vowel length.

Rilke, Rainer Maria, 'Campagna romana', in *Poesie*, tr. Andreina Lavagetto (Turin: Einaudi, 2000), 202. First published in 1908.

Melville, Herman, 'Journal 1856-57', in *The Writings of Herman Melville*, vol. 15 (Evanston and Chicago: Northwestern University Press and Newberry Library, 1989).

Hawthorne, Nathaniel. *The French and Italian Journals*, ed. Thomas Woodson (Columbus: Ohio State University Press, 1980).

10.

Pasolini, 'Una vitalità disperata, in Pasolini (2001), 113.

Galás, Diamanda, *Defixiones, Will and Testament* (London: Mute Records, 2003) [2 CD's].

Cascella, 'Diamanda Galás. La Serpenta canta ancora', *Blow Up*, 67 (2003), 22-29.

Pasolini, 'Supplica a mia madre', in Pasolini (2001), 27.

Galàs, 'Supplica a mia madre', in *Malediction and Prayer* (San Francisco: Asphodel Records, 1998) [CD].

Pasolini (2001), 24.

CHAPTER 3

1.

Gadda, Carlo Emilio, *Quer pasticciaccio brutto di via Merulana* (Milan: Garzanti, 1987), 178-179. First published in 1957.

2.

Gadda, *La cognizione del dolore* (Milan: Garzanti, 1997). First published partially as a series of instalments in the *Letteratura* journal between 1938 and 1941. First published as a volume in 1963.

3.

Gadda (1987).

Gadda, 'Impossibilità di un diario di guerra', in *Il castello di Udine* (Milan: Garzanti, 1999). Article first published in 1931. Book first published in 1934.

4.

Pavese, Cesare, *Il mestiere di vivere. Diari* (Turin: Einaudi, 2000). First published in 1952.

Melville, 'Journal 1856-57' (1989).

Pavese, 'I mari del Sud', in *Lavorare stanca* (Turin: Einaudi, 1943), 9. First published in 1936.

Mamma Roma, dir. Pasolini (1962).

Pasolini (2001), 24.

Pavese, 'Il mestiere di poeta', in *Lavorare stanca*, 129.

Pavese, *Introduzione a Moby-Dick o la balena* (Turin: Frassinelli, 1932).

5.

Melville (1989).

Pasolini (2007), 51, 58.

CHAPTER 4

A.

Melville, *Pierre, or, the Ambiguities* (London: Penguin Classics, 1996), 304-305. First published in 1852.

B.

Melville, *Moby-Dick, or, the Whale* (London: Penguin, 2003), 266. First published in 1851.

Melville, 'Letter to Nathaniel Hawthorne, June 1851', in Davis, Merrel R. and Gilman, William H., eds., *The Letters of Herman Melville* (New Haven: Yale University Press, 1960).

Gadda, 'Come lavoro', in *I viaggi la morte* (Milan: Garzanti, 2001), 10-11. First published in 1950.

C.

Melville (1996), 339, 285.

D.

Manganelli, Giorgio, 'Fregoli', in *Le interviste impossibili* (Milan: Adelphi, 1997), 120-129. First published as *A e B* in 1975.

Melville, *The Confidence-Man, His Masquerade* (New York: The Modern Library, 2003). First published in 1857.

E.

Melville (1996), 70.

Part 11
CHAPTER 5

5.
Pavese (2000).

4.

Pavese, 'La terra e la morte (1945-1946), in *Poesie del disamore* (Turin: Einaudi, 1962), 63-64. First published in 1947.

Melville, 'Daniel Orme', in *Billy Budd, Sailor and Other Stories* (London: Penguin, 1985), 413-417. First published in 1948.

It's been argued that the title and the end of *Daniel Orme* echo the last lines in the *Book of Daniel* – which apparently Melville was reading at the time – with their sense of foreboding: *Shut up the words, and seal the book.*

3.
Gadda (2001).

2.
Manganelli, *La letteratura come menzogna* (Milan: Adelphi, 1985). First published in 1967.
Manganelli, *Il rumore sottile della prosa* (Milan: Adelphi, 1994). A collection of articles published between 1966 and 1990.
Manganelli, 'Apologo sul destino della letteratura', in Manganelli (1994), 48-56.
Melville (1996), 304-305.

1.
Manganelli, 'Così noti così clandestini', in Manganelli (1994), 81-84.

CHAPTER 6

10.
Pasolini (2001), 24.
Walser, Robert, 'Music', in *Masquerade and Other Stories*, tr. Susan Bernofsky (London: Quartet Books, 1993), 9-10. First published in 1902.
Toop, David, *Sinister Resonance. The Mediumship of the Listener* (New York and London: Continuum, 2010), 53.
Simmel, Georg, 'The Philosophy of Landscape', tr. Josef Bleicher, *Theory, Culture & Society* [online journal], (2007), http://tcs.sagepub.com/content/24/7-8/20.citation accessed 24 May 2011. First published in 1913.

9.

Ø (1994).

Cascella, 'Pan Sonic. Le radici e le ali', in *Blow Up*, 74/75 (2004), 24-27.

Cascella, 'Let The Sound Flow', in *Mika Vainio. Time Examined* (Berlin: raster-noton, (2009).

Haino, Keiji, *A Challenge to Fate* (Nancy: Les Disques Du Soleil Et De L'Acier, 1994) [CD].

8.

Calvino, Italo, 'Un re in ascolto', in *Sotto il sole giaguaro* (Milan: Garzanti, 1986).

The Italian philosopher Adriana Cavarero recently wrote a detailed analysis of this story with regards to the relational nature of what she calls 'the vocalic'; that is, the sounding quality of a voice before its semantic connotations.

Cavarero, Adriana, *For More Than One Voice. Toward A Philosophy Of Vocal Expression*, tr. Paul A. Kottman (Stanford: Stanford University Press, 2005).

O'Connor, Flannery, *The Violent Bear It Away* (New York: Farrar, Straus and Giroux, 2007). First published in 1960.

O'Connor, *Mystery and Manners. Occasional Prose* (New York: Farrar, Straus and Giroux, 1969).

7.

Part of this section is a reworking of a text originally commissioned by Cathy Lane and Angus Carlyle at CRiSAP, University of the Arts London for a forthcoming anthology on listening as a practice and a methodology.

Pasolini (2007), 50.

Swinburne, Algernon Charles, 'The Nightingale', in Maxwell, Catherine, ed., *Swinburne: Selected Poems* (London: J.M. Dent, 1997), 3.

Plato, 'Phaedrus', in *Phaedrus and the Seventh and Eighth Letters*, tr.

Maxwell Hamilton (Harmondsworth: Penguin, 1973), 70.
Watson (1996).

6.

An earlier version of this text was first published in Cascella, *Some Possible Landscapes* (London: SoundFjord, 2011), a brochure accompanying Steve Roden's residency. Used with kind permission.

Roden, Steve. 'Vascellum', in LaBelle, Brandon and Roden, Steve, eds., *Site of Sound: of Architecture and the Ear* (Los Angeles: Errant Bodies Press, 1999), 116-117.

Cascella, 'Steve Roden', *Blow Up*, 22 (2000), 66-69.

Roden, *in be tween noise* [website], www.inbetweennoise.com accessed 23 May 2011.

Roden, *Airforms Archive* [blog], http://inbetweennoise. blogspot.com/ accessed 12 May 2011.

Roden, *Speak No More About the Leaves* (Lisbon: sirr.records, 2003) [CD].

5.

Latour, Bruno, 'Circulating Reference', in *Pandora's Hope. Essays on the Reality of Science Studies* (Cambridge and London: Harvard University Press, 1999), 24-79.

Latour, November, Valerie and Camacho-Hübner, Eduardo, 'Entering a Risky Territory: Space in the Age of Digital Navigation', *Environment and Planning D: Society and Space,* 28 (2010), 581-599.

Melville (2003), 266.

4.

Part of this text is directly inspired by Manganelli, 'E Sallustio non va bene?', in Manganelli (1994), 213-216.

Kraftwerk, *The Man-Machine* (Düsseldorf: Kling Klang, 1978) [LP].

Il Nuovo Canzoniere Italiano (1964).

Il Coro della S.A.T (1958).

3.

Guidi, Chiara, *Relazione sulla verità retrograda della voce*. A three-hour workshop on exploring one's voice, that Guidi has been leading for the last two years drawing on her work diaries and notebooks.

Cotten, Elizabeth, *Freight Train and Other North Carolina Folk Songs and Tunes* (Washington DC: Smithsonian Folkways, 1989) [CD].

Hopkins, Gerard Manley, *Selected Prose and Poems* (London: Penguin, 1953).

2.

Cooper, Mike, *Rayon Hula* (Rome: Hipshot Records, 2004) [CD-r].

Cascella, 'Mike Cooper. Cruising Paradise', *Blow Up*, 104 (2007), 54-58.

1.

Cascella, 'Keith Rowe. Un velo di suono', *Blow Up*, 91 (2005), 56-61.

Rowe, Keith and Tilbury, John, *Duos for Doris* (Jersey City: Erstwhile Records, 2003) [2 CD's].

Proust, Marcel, *Dalla parte di Swann* (Milan: Biblioteca Universale Rizzoli, 1985), 231.

CHAPTER 7

8.

Longhi, Roberto, 'Fatti di Masolino e Masaccio e altri studi sul Quattrocento, 1910-1967', in *Opere vol VIII/I* (Florence: Sansoni, 1975). First published in 1940.

Mamma Roma (1962).

Pasolini, *La meglio gioventù* (Florence: Sansoni, 1954).

7.
Huysmans, Joris-Karl (1972).

6.
Il Coro della S.A.T. (1958).
Ungaretti (1996).

5.
Ungaretti (1996).

4.
Baziotes, William, 'The Artist and His Mirror', *Right Angle*, 2 (6) (1949).

Baziotes, 'Statement, ca. 1957', in *William Baziotes. Late Work 1946-1962* (New York: The Marlborough Gallery, 1971).

Baziotes, 'I cannot evolve any concrete theory', *Possibilities 1* (1) (1947-48), 2.

Paneth, Donald, *William Baziotes. A Literary Portrait*, [microfilm], William and Ethel Baziotes Papers (New York: Archives of American Art, Smithsonian Institution).

Baziotes, *Letter to Alfred H. Barr, April 26, 1949*, [photocopy], Baziotes file (New York: Museum of Modern Art Library).

Sawin, Martica, 'The Cycloptic Eye, Pataphysics and the Possible: Transformations of Surrealism', in Schimmel, Paul, *The Interpretive Link, Abstract Surrealism to Abstract Expressionism* (Newport Harbor: Newport Harbor Art Museum, 1986), 37-42.

2.
Melville (1996), 70.

1.
Baziotes, Cage, John and Motherwell, Robert, *Possibilities 1*, 1 (1947) (New York: Wittenborn & Schultz).

Part 111
CHAPTER 8

1.
Marini (1979).

2.
de Martino, Ernesto, *Morte e pianto rituale nel mondo antico. Dal lamento funebre antico al pianto di Maria* (Turin: Bollati Boringhieri, 2000). First published in 1958.
de Martino, *Il mondo magico* (Turin: Bollati Boringhieri, 2007). First published in 1948.
Pasolini, ed., *Canzoniere Italiano* (Milano: Garzanti, 2006). First published in 1955.
Pasolini, 'Il canto popolare', in Pasolini (2007), 13-16.
La ricotta (1963).

3.
de Martino (2000).
da Todi, Jacopone, *Stabat Mater Dolorosa*, tr. Fr. Edward Caswall [website], http://www.preces-latinae.org/thesaurus/BVM/SMDolorosa.html accessed 22 June 2011.

4.
Marini (1979).
Pasolini (2011), 113.
Melville (1985), 413-417.

5.
Borrelli, Antonio, 'San Donato di Arezzo', in *Santi e Beati* (2002)

[website], http://www.santiebeati.it/dettaglio/33900 accessed 12 May 2011.

Benjamin, Walter, *The Translator's Task*, tr. Steven Rendall, *TTR* (1997) [online], http://id.erudit.org/iderudit/037302ar accessed 16 May 2011. First published in 1923.

CHAPTER 9

*

Pasolini (2007), 50.

Selected Bibliography

Argan, Giulio Carlo, *Immagine e persuasione. Saggi sul Barocco* (Milan: Feltrinelli, 1986).

— *L'architettura barocca in Italia* (Milan: Garzanti, 1957).

— 'La Retorica e l'arte barocca', in AA.VV., *Retorica e Barocco, Atti del III Convegno Internazionale di Studi Umanistici Venezia 1954* (Rome, 1955), 167-76.

— *Storia dell'arte italiana*, vol. III (Florence: Sansoni, 1988). First published in 1968.

Baziotes, William, Cage, John and Motherwell, Robert, *Possibilities 1*, 1 (1947) (New York: Wittenborn & Schultz).

Benjamin, Walter, *The Translator's Task*, tr. Steven Rendall (1997), *TTR* [online journal], http://id.erudit.org/iderudit/037302ar accessed 16 May 2011. First published in 1923.

Bermani, Cesare, *Pane, rose e libertà. Le canzoni che hanno fatto l'Italia: 150 anni di musica popolare, sociale e di protesta* (Milan: Biblioteca Universale Rizzoli, 2011). [Book+3CD's].

Calvino, Italo, 'Un re in ascolto', in *Sotto il sole giaguaro* (Milan: Garzanti, 1986).

Cavarero, Adriana, 'The Necessary Other', in *Relating Narratives. Storytelling and Selfhood*, tr. Paul A. Kottman (Oxon and New York: Routledge, 2000), 81-93.

Clifford, James, 'On Ethnographic Self-Fashioning', in *The Predicament of Culture* (Cambridge and London: Harvard University Press, 1988), 92-113.

Collins, Wilkie, *Armadale* (London: Penguin Books, 2004). First published in 1864.

— *The Woman in White* (London: Penguin Books, 2002). First published in 1866.

da Todi, Jacopone, *Stabat Mater Dolorosa*, tr. Fr. Edward Caswall [website], http://www.preces-latinae.org/thesaurus/BVM/SM Dolorosa.html accessed 22 June 2011.

de Martino, Ernesto, *Morte e pianto rituale nel mondo antico. Dal lamento funebre antico al pianto di Maria* (Turin: Bollati Boringhieri, 2000). First published in 1958.

Didion, Joan, 'The Art of Nonfiction', in *The Paris Review Interviews*, vol. 1 (Edinburgh: Canongate, 2007), 473-500.

— *The White Album* (New York: Farrar, Straus and Giroux, 1979).

Gadda, Carlo Emilio, *Il castello di Udine* (Milan: Garzanti, 1999). First published in 1934.

— *I viaggi la morte* (Milan: Garzanti, 2001). First published in 1950.

— *La cognizione del dolore* (Milan: Garzanti, 1997). First published partially as a series of instalments in the *Letteratura* journal between 1938 and 1941. First published as a volume in 1963.

— *Quer pasticciaccio brutto di via Merulana* (Milan: Garzanti, 1987). First published in 1957.

Gramsci, Antonio, *Quaderni del carcere* (XVIII), ed. Felice Platone (Turin: Einaudi 1948-1951).

Hawthorne, Nathaniel. *The French and Italian Journals,* ed. Thomas Woodson (Columbus: Ohio State University Press, 1980).

Hopkins, Gerard Manley, *Selected Prose and Poems* (London: Penguin Books, 1953).

Huysmans, Joris-Karl, *Là-bas,* tr. Keene Wallace (New York: Dover Publications 1972). First published in 1891.

Jankélévitch, Vladimir, *Music and the Ineffable,* tr. Carolyn Abbate (Princeton and Oxford: Princeton University Press, 2003). First published in 1961.

Kierkegaard, Søren, *Repetition* and *Philosophical Crumbs,* tr. M.G. Piety (Oxford: Oxford University Press, 2009). First published in 1843.

Kubin, Alfred, *The Other Side,* tr. Mike Mitchell (Sawtry: Dedalus Ltd., 2000). First published in 1909.

Latour, Bruno, 'Circulating Reference', in *Pandora's Hope. Essays on the Reality of Science Studies* (Cambridge and London: Harvard University Press, 1999), 24-79.

— November, Valerie and Camacho-Hübner, Eduardo, 'Entering a Risky Territory: Space in the Age of Digital Navigation', *Environment and Planning D: Society and Space*, 28 (2010), 581-599.

Levi, Carlo, *Roma fuggitiva. Scritti 1951-1963* (Rome: Donzelli, 2011).

Longhi, Roberto, 'Fatti di Masolino e Masaccio e altri studi sul Quattrocento, 1910-1967', in *Opere vol VIII/I* (Florence: Sansoni, 1975). First published in 1940.

Manganelli, Giorgio, 'Fregoli', in *Le interviste impossibili* (Milan: Adelphi, 1997), 120-129. First published as *A e B* in 1975.

— *Il rumore sottile della prosa* (Milan: Adelphi, 1994). A collection of articles published between 1966 and 1990.

— *La letteratura come menzogna* (Milan: Adelphi, 1985). First published in 1967.

Melville, Herman. 'Daniel Orme', in *Billy Budd, Sailor and Other Stories* (London: Penguin, 1985), 413-417. First published in 1948.

— 'Journal 1856-57', in *The Writings of Herman Melville*, vol. 15 (Evanston and Chicago: Northwestern University Press and Newberry Library, 1989).

— *Moby-Dick, or, The Whale* (London: Penguin Classics, 2003). First published in 1851.

— *Moby-Dick o la balena*, translated, with an introduction by Cesare Pavese (Turin: Frassinelli, 1932).

— *Pierre, or, The Ambiguities* (London: Penguin Classics, 1996). First published in 1852.

— *The Confidence-Man, His Masquerade* (New York: The Modern Library, 2003). First published in 1857.

O'Connor, Flannery, *Mystery and Manners. Occasional Prose* (New York: Farrar, Straus and Giroux, 1969).

— *The Violent Bear It Away* (New York: Farrar, Straus and

Giroux, 2007). First published in 1960.

Olson, Charles, *Call Me Ishmael* (San Francisco: City Lights Books, 1947).

Pasolini, Pier Paolo, ed., *Canzoniere Italiano* (Milano: Garzanti, 2006). First published in 1955.

— *Le ceneri di Gramsci* (Milan: Garzanti, 2007). First published in 1957.

— *Poesia in forma di rosa* (Milan: Garzanti, 2001). First published in 1964.

Pavese, Cesare, *Il mestiere di vivere. Diari* (Turin: Einaudi, 2000). First published in 1952.

— 'La terra e la morte, 1945-1946', in *Poesie del disamore* (Turin: Einaudi, 1962), 63-64. First published in 1947.

— *Lavorare stanca* (Turin: Einaudi, 1943). First published in 1936.

Proust, Marcel, *Alla ricerca del tempo perduto*, vols. I-VII (Turin: Einaudi, 1978). First published between 1913 and 1927.

Richter, Jean Paul, *Il discorso del Cristo Morto e altri sogni*, tr. Bruna Bianchi (Milan: SE, 1997). First published in 1796.

Riegl, Alois, *The Origins of Baroque Art in Rome*, trs. Andrew Hopkins and Arnold Witte (Los Angeles: Getty Publications, 2010). First published in 1908.

Rilke, Rainer Maria. 'Campagna romana', in *Poesie*, tr. Andreina Lavagetto (Turin: Einaudi, 2000), 202. First published in 1908.

Roden, Steve, *Airforms Archive* [blog], http://inbetweennoise.blogspot.com/accessed 12 May 2011.

— *in be tween noise* [website], www.inbetweennoise.com accessed 23 May 2011.

Ruskin, John, 'Praeterita' and 'The Seven Lamps of Architecture: The Lamp of Memory' (1903-12), in Cook, Edward Tyas and Weddenburn, Alexander, eds., *The Library Edition of the Works of John Ruskin* (London: George Allen, 1889), vol. 35, 562; vol. 8, 247.

Simmel, Georg, 'The Philosophy of Landscape', tr. Josef Bleicher,

Theory, Culture & Society [online journal] (2007), http://tcs.sagepub.com/content/24/7-8/20.citation accessed 24 May 2011. First published in 1913.

Straniero, Giovanni and Barletta, Mauro, *La rivolta in musica* (Turin: Lindau, 2003).

Toop, David, *Sinister Resonance. The Mediumship of the Listener* (New York and London: Continuum, 2010).

Ungaretti, Giuseppe, 'Veglia (Cima Quattro, 23 dicembre 1915)', in *Vita d'un uomo* (Milan: Meridiani Mondadori, 1996), 25.

Voegelin, Salomé, *Listening to Noise and Silence. Towards a Philosophy of Sound Art* (New York and London: Continuum, 2010).

Walser, Robert, 'Music', in *Masquerade and Other Stories*, tr. Susan Bernofsky (London: Quartet Books, 1993), 9-10. First published in 1902.

Weiss, Allen S., *Varieties of Audio Mimesis: Musical Evocations of Landscape* (Errant Bodies Press, 2008).

Wölfflin, Heinrich, *Renaissance and Baroque*, tr. Kathrin Simon (Ithaca, NY: Cornell University Press, 1967). First published in 1888.

Contemporary culture has eliminated both the concept of the public and the figure of the intellectual. Former public spaces – both physical and cultural – are now either derelict or colonized by advertising. A cretinous anti-intellectualism presides, cheerled by expensively educated hacks in the pay of multinational corporations who reassure their bored readers that there is no need to rouse themselves from their interpassive stupor. The informal censorship internalized and propagated by the cultural workers of late capitalism generates a banal conformity that the propaganda chiefs of Stalinism could only ever have dreamt of imposing. Zer0 Books knows that another kind of discourse – intellectual without being academic, popular without being populist – is not only possible: it is already flourishing, in the regions beyond the striplit malls of so-called mass media and the neurotically bureaucratic halls of the academy. Zer0 is committed to the idea of publishing as a making public of the intellectual. It is convinced that in the unthinking, blandly consensual culture in which we live, critical and engaged theoretical reflection is more important than ever before.